TWENTY-FIRST-CENTURY KIDS,
TWENTY-FIRST-CENTURY
LIBRARIANS

VIRGINIA A. WALTER

AMERICAN LIBRARY ASSOCIATION

Chicago   2010

Virginia A. Walter holds a BA in world literature, an MLIS from the University of California, Berkeley, and a PhD in public administration from the University of Southern California. Before joining the faculty in what is now the Information Studies Department at UCLA in 1990, she had worked for more than twenty years in public libraries, most recently as children's services coordinator at Los Angeles Public Library. She retired in June 2008 with the rank of professor emerita. She is the author of two books for young people, nine monographs, and more than thirty-five articles in scholarly and professional journals.

While extensive effort has gone into ensuring the reliability of information appearing in this book, the publisher makes no warranty, express or implied, on the accuracy or reliability of the information, and does not assume and hereby disclaims any liability to any person for any loss or damage caused by errors or omissions in this publication.

The paper used in this publication meets the minimum requirements of American National Standard for Information Sciences—Permanence of Paper for Printed Library Materials, ANSI Z39.48-1992. ∞

Library of Congress Cataloging-in-Publication Data

Walter, Virginia A.
    Twenty-first-century kids, twenty-first-century librarians / Virginia A. Walter.
        p.   cm.
    Includes bibliographical references and index.
    ISBN 978-0-8389-1007-8 (alk. paper)
    1. Children's libraries—United States. 2. Young adults' libraries—United States. 3. Children's librarians—United States. 4. Young adult services librarians—United States. I. Title.
    Z718.2.U6W358 2010
    027.62'5—dc22
                                       2009016972

ISBN-13: 978-0-8389-1007-8

Printed in the United States of America

14 13 12 11 10   5 4 3 2 1

CONTENTS

PREFACE

I LOOK BACK NOW ON A LONG CAREER THAT HAS BEEN CENTERED ON children and libraries. I have watched as committed, caring, thoughtful children's librarians shifted their attention from books to computers and back to books again. I have watched as they took on new roles as literacy coaches for parents of young children and creators of after-school home-work centers for latchkey kids. I have cheered them on as they learned the new skills of outcome evaluation and the new language of information literacy. I learned from them as they have sometimes learned from me.

When I sat down to write *Children and Libraries: Getting It Right* (2001) at the end of the twentieth century, I thought those would be my last words on the subject. To my surprise, the world has changed and so have I. Our profession is so rich with tradition and potential that we may never run out of new ways to think about it and new ways to practice it.

This is not simply a revised and expanded edition of that earlier book although it does revisit some of the original content. It is a new book that has been inspired by a new generation of children's librarians and by the old veterans who continue to get it right. This is a new book for a new time.

Chapter 1 looks again at the history of library services to children in the United States. Chapter 2 begins a reconsideration of the legacy passed on to us by the founders of our profession, and chapter 3 examines more recent trends and issues. Chapter 4 is in many ways the heart of the book. It presents five constructs or models of childhood—the child reader, the child of the information age, the child in the community, the global child, and the empowered child—and invites you to think about how each of these concepts could inform the way we provide service to children today and into the future. Chapter 5 summarizes some manage-ment and leadership strategies that could help us get it right for children. Chapter 6 both wraps it all up and suggests a new beginning.

For many years now, I have been inspired by the words of a traditional greeting among the Masai people of Africa. As the story goes, when one Masai warrior meets another, he asks, "How are the children?" The traditional response is, "All the children are well."

All of us in the community that supports children and libraries yearn for the day when we can honestly reply, "All the children are well." That is why we do what we do. Here is a book to sustain you until that day arrives.

ACKNOWLEDGMENTS

I RESPECTFULLY ACKNOWLEDGE AND THANK

The UCLA students who have challenged me, stimulated me, and reassured me that the profession of children's librarians will be in good hands into the foreseeable future.

The many children's librarians around the country who have shared their experiences with me, offered their libraries as research sites, and provided multiple reality checks to my professorial theorizing.

My daughter, Eva Mitnick, second-generation children's librarian, who gets it right and does it better than I ever dreamed possible.

Susan Patron, Theresa Nelson, and Lucy Frank—friends who write and ladies who lunch.

Elaine Meyers, my sometime coauthor, intellectual companion, and dear friend, who always makes me go back and think again.

Where We Came From

Beginnings

WHEN PHILANTHROPISTS AND CIVIC LEADERS ESTABLISHED THE FIRST public libraries in the early 1800s, their intentions were to provide good reading for adults who were not wealthy enough to purchase their own books and to help assimilate immigrants from Europe into American society. The policy makers put it like this when they developed a mission statement for the new Boston Public Library in 1852: "There can be no doubt that . . . reading ought to be furnished to all, on the same principle that we furnish free education" (Williams 1988, 4). From the beginning, there was a conviction that books and reading are essential to the human spirit. In 1950, Robert D. Leigh looked back on the foundations of the public library and called its ideological underpinning the "library faith," "a belief in the virtue of the printed word, especially of the book, the reading of which is held to be good in itself or from its reading flows that which is good" (Leigh 1950, 12). Indeed, librarians needed to be true believers because there was no empirical proof of the benefits of uplifting reading.

With very few exceptions, those early libraries with their shelves of high-minded literature were not open to children. However, at the end of the nineteenth century, this practice began to change. William I. Fletcher was one of the early advocates for extending public library service to young people. In 1876, the U.S. Bureau of Education commissioned a study of the "history, condition, and management" of public libraries. In a chapter devoted to the topic of public libraries and the young, Fletcher argued forcibly that libraries should change their policies limiting access by children. He based his argument on the very "library faith" that had guided the establishment of the first public libraries: people should develop good reading habits and a taste for refined reading early in life. He wrote:

If there is any truth in the idea that the public library is not merely a storehouse for the supply of the wants of the reading public, but also and especially an educational institution which shall create wants where they do not exist, then the library ought to bring its influence to bear on the young as early as possible. (414)

Fletcher warned that if librarians do not reach children while they are young, they will develop a taste for light reading—dime novels and cheap stories. Libraries, he insisted, should provide children with good books that are "instructive and stimulating to the better nature" (416). His passionate message was consistent with other ideas beginning to circulate at that time about the need to reach children early in their lives in order to influence the kind of adults they would become.

During the last two decades of the nineteenth century, the ideas of some new experts in child studies began to spread to other disciplines. John Dewey's ideas about education and G. Stanley Hall's theories about child psychology were particularly influential. The Child Study Association was established and became a forum for interdisciplinary discussion of children's social, physical, emotional, and educational needs (Wishy 1968, 107). Professionals with a particular concern for children emerged in the fields of education, social work, child psychology, and librarianship. This concern, combined with the optimism and the crusading spirit of reform that permeated that age, gave birth to new hope. If children could be nurtured properly, said the experts of that time, perhaps they would grow up to take their places in a better society (Hawes 1991, 26–27).

Librarians, for their part, were convinced that children who were exposed to fine, uplifting literature would grow up to be fine, uplifted adults. Betsy Hearne describes the work of the pioneers of children's library services as a visionary quest in which the "grail was not just information or even knowledge but the enrichment of experience through whole reading, the kind of reading that engulfs the heart as well as engaging the head and ultimately shapes a lifetime" (Hearne and Jenkins 1999, 538). Those early children's librarians were true believers in the "library faith."

Little by little, libraries began to open their doors to children. Perhaps influenced by the principles of the progressive movement, public libraries followed in the path of social welfare and recreation services, the justice system, and public health programs and began to offer specialized services for children (Jenkins 1996). By the end of the nineteenth century, children were welcome in a number of libraries across the country—among them Minneapolis, Minnesota; Hartford, Connecticut; Denver, Colorado; and San Francisco, California. In 1896, the Pratt Institute in Brooklyn and the Providence Public Library in Rhode Island opened buildings that featured dedicated children's rooms designed for young library users (Thomas 1990).

Anne Carroll Moore, one of the first librarians to work in the children's room at the Pratt Institute, described it as an attractive space furnished with chairs and tables designed with children's physical comfort in mind. The shelves were filled with beautiful art books that had been created for adults because as yet there were few books published especially for children. The children's room was intended to be a welcoming, homelike, familiar place filled with art, flowers, and growing plants as well as books. It was a place where children, many of whom lived in crowded, dingy tenement buildings, could be surrounded by beautiful objects that would inspire their wonder. Moore wrote, "[F]rom the low windows, children and grown people looked out upon a terraced playground down which the children rolled and tumbled in summer and coasted in winter" (1969, 66). She makes it sound like paradise.

Frances Jenkins Olcott, the head of the children's department of the Carnegie Library of Pittsburgh, described the functions of the children's room in her report to the American Library Association meeting in Portland, Oregon, in 1905:

> The ideal children's room has a double function. First, it is the place in which the children are being prepared to use the adult library, and we feel that if our rooms fail to develop intelligent, self-helpful readers, we have failed in our main object. Second, the ideal children's room should *take the place of a child's private library*, and it should, as far as possible, give the child a chance to browse among books of all classes and kinds, in a room beautifully proportioned and decorated, and presided over by a genial and sympathetic woman who has a genuine interest in the personalities and preferences of the boys and girls. (73)

As public libraries began to offer books and services for children, they also began to recognize the need for specialist staff—the "genial and sympathetic wom[e]n [with] a genuine interest in the . . . preferences of the boys and girls"—to provide for this new clientele. In 1905, Olcott described the characteristics of the ideal applicant to the training school for children's librarians that had been established at the Carnegie Library:

> Sympathy with and respect for children, strength of character, a genial nature, a pleasing personality, an instinct for reading character, adaptability, and last but not least, a strong sense of humor. Her home training and education should have given her a love and knowledge of books, a fund of general information, a quick and accurate mind. These qualities are difficult to find combined in one person. (75)

Mary Wright Plummer presumably found the right candidates for the job because she hired children's librarians for the Pratt Institute in Brooklyn as early as 1902; and in 1906, Anne Carroll Moore was chosen to supervise children's services at the New York Public Library. She remained there as superintendent of work with children until she retired in 1941 (Sayers 1972). Other young women were also attracted to this field that allowed them to combine a love of reading with the nurturing of children. In a presentation at the annual conference of the American Library Association in 1913, Arthur Bostwick commended children's work as the first specialization within the profession of librarianship and urged that even more specialized training for children's librarians be provided (Bostwick 1913). Pratt Institute had begun offering lectures on children's library work in 1896, and the Carnegie Library in Pittsburgh offered a training class for children's librarians in 1900. This class developed into a school that trained children's librarians exclusively, providing a cadre of children's librarians who became early leaders in the field (Fenwick 1976, 341).

Anne Carroll Moore probably did more than anyone in those early years to define and institutionalize public library services for children. By all accounts, she was a remarkable person. In her scholarly account of the remarkable women who shaped the modern children's book industry between 1919 and 1939, Jacalyn Eddy writes, "Anne Carroll Moore has been variously described as a shepherdess, the godmother of fairy books, a pioneer, a world citizen, a commander in chief, and a comrade in arms" (2006, 30). If she had been a man in that era when arenas for women's accomplishments were severely limited, she could have made significant contributions in any number of fields. Margaret K. McElderry (1997) reveals that Moore had planned to become a lawyer like her father, but when he died she was no longer able to clerk in his office and had to look elsewhere for a career. Fortunately for our field, she found library work.

Mentored by Mary Wright Plummer and Caroline Hewins, she became an advocate for children early in her library career.

Moore's accomplishments at the New York Public Library were extraordinary. She believed that the library should be an inviting, gracious environment for children. As she opened children's rooms in successive branch libraries, she made sure they were attractive and welcoming to young people. She established noncirculating collections of fine children's books to ensure that young library patrons would always be able to read and appreciate great literature in the library. She worked to liberalize circulation policies for young patrons and to expand services to include story hours and cooperative efforts with schools. She developed the children's room at the library's flagship building at Fifth Avenue and 42nd Street into a cultural mecca with an international reputation among writers and illustrators of books for children (Lundin 1998).

Moore believed that the public library could contribute to the socialization of children as well as to their literary development. She instituted a pledge that all children signed when they got their library cards: "When I write my name in this book I promise to take good care of the books I use at home" (Sayers 1972, 68). In this way, children learned their responsibilities as library users and as citizens participating in a civic activity. When I was a children's librarian at San Francisco Public Library in the early 1960s, one of my tasks was to administer a similar pledge to children before they could receive their library cards. We did not inspect their hands for cleanliness before they could handle the books, however, a practice not unknown in the early days of children's services.

Julie Cummins has observed that Anne Carroll Moore developed her approach to library service to children through exploration of both educational and social service philosophies and practices. She codified her philosophy of children's services as the "Four Respects," which she communicated to the children's librarians whom she trained. The first was respect for children. Second was respect for children's books. Third was respect for children's librarians as an integral element in the library's organization. Fourth was respect for the professional status of children's librarianship, which Moore herself worked tirelessly to elevate (Cummins 1999, 27).

Anne Carroll Moore exerted her influence in the publishing community as well as in the domain of professional librarians. Barbara Bader (1997) notes that Moore and her associates "created the world of children's books as a sodality, a community of interest, and the field of children's literature as a specialty" (520). Through her strategic position in

New York City, Moore developed personal and professional friendships with editors such as Louise Seaman Bechtel and with children's book authors such as Leslie Brooke, Padraic Colum, Walter de la Mare, and Beatrix Potter.

Moore also wrote reviews of children's books for the respected literary journal *The Bookman* from 1918 to 1926; and in 1924, she instituted a regular column called "The Three Owls" for the *New York Herald Tribune*. Leonard Marcus writes that during this early period, she regularly hounded the major New York publishers to take the production of children's books seriously (2008, 72–73). Moore continued the Three Owls tradition and logo in regular contributions to *Horn Book* from 1936 to 1960 (Vandergrift 1996, 694). Her legacy of sustained criticism of children's literature was an important contribution to the children's book trade, which was developing simultaneously with the growth of children's library services. Writing consistently in the most influential reviewing media of her time, Moore acquired a certain reputation, not always appreciated by people in the publishing world who disagreed with her opinion, as a "taste maker" in the world of children's literature. As Bader points out, her reviews were not intended to be merely guidance for the lay reader; they were also meant to influence the editor, the publisher, the author, and the entire children's literature community.

Anne Carroll Moore was succeeded by Frances Clarke Sayers at New York Public Library. Sayers was another woman of formidable opinions and abilities. There followed, in libraries throughout the country, a long line of women who brought to children's library services the full measure of their passion, dedication, intelligence, and organizational abilities. A number of scholars (Jenkins 1996; Lundin 1996; Vandergrift 1996) have speculated on the impact that such a strong feminine (and feminist) orientation may have had on our profession. Vandergrift also notes that many of the early leaders in children's librarianship were African American—Augusta Baker, Charlemae Rollins, and Barbara Rollock, to name a few. The overall significance of their contributions has not yet been assessed, but they were certainly responsible for raising awareness about the multicultural and multiracial nature of the children we serve and the need for more sensitive and less stereotyped books to share with children of all races.

Looking at the canon of influential professional literature contributed by the early young people's librarians, their protégés, and colleagues in related fields—Annis Duff, Margaret A. Edwards, Paul Hazard, Bertha E. Mahony, Anne Carroll Moore, Amelia H. Munson, Ruth Sawyer,

Frances Clarke Sayers, Marie L. Shedlock, Lillian Smith, and Ruth Hill Viguers—Christine Jenkins finds seven articles of faith that permeate the writings:

1. A belief in the primacy and uniqueness of the individual child
2. A belief in the critical importance of individual choice in young people's reading
3. A firm belief in the strength and resilience of young people
4. A belief in the children's room as an egalitarian republic of readers
5. A belief in literature as a positive force for understanding not only between individuals but also between groups and nations
6. A friendly and unsentimental older sister's attitude toward children
7. An assumption that children's librarians would prevail over adversity in the performance of their professional work (Hearne and Jenkins 1999, 552–58)

Although these core beliefs are part of the heritage and ideology of most librarians working with children today, it can be argued that the strength of their conviction has diminished. Few contemporary children's librarians approach their work with the same passion and near-religious fervor the pioneers of our profession exuded. As Jenkins writes, "Invested in both communion and crusade, the foremothers of children's librarianship created a new testament of faith in the miraculous powers of the word" (Hearne and Jenkins 1999, 558).

Expansion

The early innovators of children's librarianship were aided in their efforts to institutionalize the service by an unlikely ally—Andrew Carnegie. Among the steel magnate's most lasting philanthropic contributions were the Carnegie libraries, built throughout the United States from 1886 to 1917. These libraries were all designed for efficient circulation of reading materials, and nearly all of them allocated space especially for children. The original guidelines for these children's rooms called for orderly rows of tables and chairs that were meant to encourage orderly reading behavior. Children's librarians, however, soon modified the guidelines and created more child-friendly environments (Van Slyck 1995).

In 1929, the American Library Association's Committee on Library Work with Children published the *Children's Library Yearbook*, which was intended to be an annual publication. I can find no record that a second volume was ever published; it may have been a casualty of the Great Depression. This first yearbook, nevertheless, is a fascinating record of the progress that had been made in institutionalizing library service to children in a few decades. In an opening statement, Linda A. Eastman (1929) applauds the achievements that had been made:

> Following the first stages of experimentation with separate children's rooms, there were gradually worked out the present recognized requirements for the equipment of such rooms, the formulation of standards for selection of juvenile books, the principles and methods of work with children, and perhaps most important of all the training of children's librarians. (1)

Effie L. Power, who had written a well-received text for educating children's librarians, contributed a chapter in the yearbook on "The Equipment of a Children's Room." In addition to listing the requisite "low shelving, furniture adapted to children's stature, space in which to move about freely, an orderly and inviting arrangement of carefully selected books and a trained children's librarian," she includes guidelines for heating, lighting, ventilation, and floor covering. She indicates standard sizes for tables and chairs and suggests that window seats are useful and can cover radiators. She notes that benches without backs are both uncomfortable and unhygienic (Power 1929, 16ff). She doesn't cite her sources or influences, but the prevailing scientific management principles of the time are obvious.

One appendix in the yearbook gives salary statistics; another provides the curricula of library schools that specialized in library work with children. However, much of the yearbook is devoted to book selection and discussion of the importance of reading in the lives of children. Frederic G. Melcher (1929) acknowledges the efforts of children's librarians in promoting children's reading and thereby encouraging the development of the children's book publishing industry. Anne Carroll Moore is even more direct. She opens her essay by noting the tremendous changes in children's book production that had occurred in the previous ten years. She asks why these changes had occurred and then provides the answer: "It may readily be traced, I think, to the general abandonment of an age limit in public libraries just before the turn of the century and the wider recognition of children's tastes in reading as a subject worthy of specialized study and organization" (Moore 1929, 22). She goes on to rhapsodize about the phenomenon of children mixing and mingling in the library where they are exposed to children's books and where they can voluntarily choose which ones they want to read.

By the end of the 1920s, then, American public libraries had a philosophy of children's services that had been articulated by the visionary founding mothers. They also had dedicated space set aside for children in the Carnegie buildings that had sprung up all over the country. Sara Innis Fenwick (1976) points out that from the 1920s until the 1950s libraries throughout the United States jumped on the bandwagon and adopted the children's library practices that had been developed with such energy and innovation in the early part of the century. Not even the disrupting events of the Great Depression of the 1930s or World War II could halt the inexorable spread of children's services in public libraries. During this time of diffusion, children's services became an institutionalized part of public library offerings. Some libraries offered specialized services to young adults during this time, but no other significant changes in the structure or patterns of service for young people occurred until after World War II.

Public library services got a big boost in 1956 when the federal government passed the Library Services Act, later known as the Library Services and Construction Act (LSCA). The act funded both construction and demonstration projects. The additional money that trickled down to local communities under this legislation enabled many libraries to expand their basic services and to experiment with new kinds of programs. Libraries were also eligible for some of the War on Poverty programs of the Johnson administration. There was an impetus to reach new populations, to "serve the unserved," and *outreach* became a new buzzword in the profession (Molz and Dain 1999).

They didn't use the term *outreach*, but those earlier children's librarians had also been aware of the need to work alongside other social service agencies to meet the needs of disadvantaged children. Barbara Rollock reminds us that at the beginning of the twentieth century, children's librarians in urban areas were particularly focused on immigrant children whose parents might be reluctant to visit the library. Their objectives were to use books to help children and their families keep some link with their heritage and to assimilate into their new culture and society (Rollock 1988, 6). At the same time, librarians serving rural populations worried about how to get books into the hands of children living in remote farming communities. It wasn't until the post–World War II years, however, that dedicated federal funding was available to help librarians find ways to reach underserved populations.

During the 1960s, with national attention focused on the needs of our most disadvantaged people, outreach programs designed to take library programs outside the walls of the library to nonwhite and economically disadvantaged people who were not traditional library users became a concern of libraries everywhere. Libraries experimented with new kinds of mobile services. Outreach librarians also tried to attract new users with innovative programs ranging from tricycle races in the parking lot to African dance presentations. Children's librarians told stories to groups of kids in housing project playgrounds and at street festivals. Many libraries' book collections blossomed with more multicultural content than they ever had before (Fenwick 1976, 355–56). Unfortunately, the impact of the era of big federal aid on services to children has not been measured (Chelton 1980; Willett 1995, 94ff). Although many programs were abandoned when federal aid was withdrawn, outreach and community cooperation became established during this period as good practice for children's library services and continue in many libraries to this day.

The latest enactment of federal legislation for libraries is the Library Services and Technology Act (LSTA), authorized for the first time in 1997. As the name implies, its focus is on technology. In addition to funding the development of electronic information resources and the establishment of electronic linkages among libraries and other service providers, however, the act aims to improve the provision of library services to underserved populations. LSTA funds are allocated as follows: 91.5 percent to state library agencies that distribute them to libraries in their jurisdictions for a variety of purposes; 4 percent to competitive national leadership grants that provide for education and training of library personnel, research and demonstration projects, preservation and digitization projects, and model cooperative activities between libraries and museums; and 1.5 percent to services for Indian tribes. These programs are all administered by one agency, the Institute of Museum and Library Services (IMLS).

The Library Services and Technology Act took federal responsibility for public libraries out of the U.S. Department of Education, where it had been located for more than a hundred years (Molz and Dain 1999, 104ff). As might be expected under the administration of the new Institute of Museum and Library Services, there is a new focus on partnerships between libraries and museums. Some of the natural affinities between children's library services and children's museums have been exploited under this funding umbrella. For example, in 2006, IMLS funded a partnership between the Denver Public Library, the Denver Art Museum, and the Museo de las Americas to improve service to Spanish-speaking families (Institute of Museum and Library Services 2008).

Accountability

During the 1980s, local governments throughout the country experienced budgetary shortfalls caused by regional economic downturns and changes in tax structures such as those embodied in Proposition 13 in California. One of the responses was a renewed emphasis on documenting productivity and accountability for results in government agencies, including public libraries. The authors of an influential book from this period, *Reinventing Government: How the Entrepreneurial Spirit Is Transforming the Public Sector*, pointed out a significant governmental shift from funding inputs to funding outputs (Osborne and Gaebler 1992). Policy makers were demanding to know what kind of return they would get from their increasingly limited financial investment. Accordingly, department managers were being asked to anticipate results in their budget requests and to provide quantifiable measures of their achievements. Many library managers were forced to look beyond their traditional circulation and reference use counts for more descriptive and reliable ways to account for their outputs.

The Public Library Association (PLA), a division of the American Library Association (ALA), responded to this need for more comprehensive measurement techniques with *Output Measures for Public Libraries*, second edition (Van House et al. 1987), a companion to *Planning and Role Setting for Public Libraries* (McClure et al. 1987). These manuals, intended to be general and comprehensive, did not deal specifically with any elements of library service to children other than those associated with a role the authors called Preschoolers' Door to Learning. They presumed that libraries could adapt the planning process and measurement techniques to any specialized services that were appropriate for their organizations.

Adele Fasick (1990) has observed that children's librarians have often resented and resisted having to evaluate the services they provide. Some have argued that the most important services are intangible and unquantifiable. How does one compute the value of good books in a child's life? Some have felt defensive about having to justify the worth of a service that is chronically underfunded and undervalued. Others, however, were concerned that existing techniques for measuring general library services, such as *Output Measures for Public Libraries,* did not adequately capture the outputs of library services for children. This concern was partially mitigated by the publication of *Output Measures for Public Library Service to Children* (Walter 1992).

Output Measures for Public Library Service to Children is a manual of standardized procedures for collecting, interpreting, and using quantitative data that measure the outputs of children's services. As such, it is also a kind of snapshot of the range of services provided to children in most public libraries in the 1990s. It delineates the following output measures:

Library Use Measures

> *Children's Library Visits per Child* is the average number of visits per child to the library by people age 14 and under in the community served. It measures walk-in use of the library.

> *Building Use by Children* indicates the average number of people age 14 and under who are in the library at any particular time. Together with *Children's Library Visits per Child,* this measure shows patterns of use.

> *Furniture/Equipment Use by Children* measures the proportion of time, on average, that a particular type of furniture or equipment, such as preschool seating or computer terminals, is in use by people age 14 and under.

Materials Use Measures

> *Circulation of Children's Materials per Child* measures the number of children's library materials loaned for use outside the library, relative to the number of people age 14 and under in the service area.

> *In-Library Use of Children's Library Materials per Child* indicates the use of children's library materials within the library, relative to the number of people age 14 and under in the community served.

> *Turnover Rate of Children's Materials* indicates the intensity of use of the children's collection, relating the cir-

culation of children's materials to the total size of the children's collection.

Materials Availability Measures

Children's Fill Rate is the percentage of successful searches for library materials by users age 14 and under and adults acting on behalf of children.

Homework Fill Rate is the proportion of successful searches for information or library materials for homework use by library users age 14 and under and adults acting on behalf of children.

Picture Book Fill Rate is the percentage of successful searches for picture books.

Information Services Measures

Children's Information Transactions per Child is the number of information transactions per person age 14 and under in the community served made by those library users age 14 and under and by adults acting on their behalf.

Children's Information Transaction Completion Rate is the percentage of successful information transactions by persons age 14 and under and by adults acting on behalf of children.

Programming Measures

Children's Program Attendance per Child measures annual attendance at children's library programs per person age 14 and under in the community served. May also be customized to measure attendance at particular programs such as Summer Reading or Family Storytime.

Community Relations

Class Visit Rate measures visits from school classes to the library relative to the total number of school classes in the library.

Child Care Center Contact Rate is the number of contacts between the library and child care centers relative to the number of child care centers in the community.

Annual Number of Community Contacts is the total number of community contacts made by library staff responsible for service to children during the year.

Librarians have used the specialized output measures for children's services and a companion volume, *Output Measures and More: Planning and Evaluating Public Library Services for Young Adults* (Walter 1995), to formulate budget requests, to make informed decisions about service patterns and resource allocations, to evaluate grant-funded projects, to compare youth services to other elements in the overall program of the library, and to measure progress toward various objectives. The use of these management information tools represented a shift for many children's librarians toward accountability and a willingness to judge the effectiveness of their work. Output measures also helped to document what most children's librarians have always known—that the work of these specialists is wide ranging and produces tangible results.

The latest iteration of a planning process by the Public Library Association eliminated the Preschoolers' Door to Learning from its menu of service responses. The new list of eighteen service responses, adopted in 2007, is intended to be a more specific representation of public library responses to community needs than the more general library roles had been. The list provides a common vocabulary for a set of primary service roles or priorities that a public library might choose to offer to its community. The service responses are given in two phrases, the first describing what the user receives and the second what the library offers.

- Be an informed citizen: local, national, and world affairs
- Build successful enterprises: business and nonprofit support
- Celebrate diversity: cultural awareness
- Connect to the online world: public Internet access
- Create young readers: early literacy
- Discover your roots: genealogy and local history
- Express creativity: create and share content
- Get facts fast: ready reference
- Know your community: community resources and services
- Learn to read and write: adult, teen, and family literacy
- Make career choices: job and career development

- Make informed decisions: health, wealth, and other life choices
- Satisfy curiosity: lifelong learning
- Stimulate imagination: reading, viewing, and listening for pleasure
- Succeed in school: homework help
- Understand how to find, evaluate, and use information: information fluency
- Visit a comfortable place: physical and virtual spaces
- Welcome to the United States: new immigrants will have information on citizenship, English Language Learning (ELL), employment, public schooling, health and safety, available social services, and any other topics that they need to participate successfully in American life (Garcia and Nelson 2007, 3)

The continuing commitment of the Public Library Association to an evolving planning process is evidence of the ongoing need for management decision-making tools that can be easily used by professional librarians.

Increasingly, children's librarians demand to be seen as managers. In many libraries, a children's services coordinator is a member of the administrative team. Even children's librarians who work alone in small library agencies assume management responsibilities as they assess their communities; plan, implement, market, and evaluate programs and services; supervise pages and volunteers; manage complex multimedia collections; raise funds; and network with other youth-serving professionals. Of course, they still tell stories, provide reference and readers' advisory assistance, compile book lists and bibliographies, create bulletin board displays, teach Internet classes to children and parents, and participate in professional associations such as the Association for Library Service to Children (ALSC). It is a measure of the widespread acceptance of this concept of the children's librarian as a manager that a book published by the American Library Association in 1995, *Youth Services Librarians as Managers* (Staerkel, Fellows, and Nespeca 1995), included chapters on planning, budgeting, grantsmanship, policies and procedures, evaluation, personnel issues, recruitment, strategies for conducting effective meetings, and networking and cooperation. Although the context for these topics was library service to children, the topics themselves are suited to a general management textbook.

New Challenges

Children's librarians had barely adjusted to the consequences of the budgetary shortfalls of the 1980s when another challenge caused public library professionals to question their traditional social role and mission. This challenge was the digital revolution created by the personal computer and the rapid increase in individual access to the Internet. The challenge was often framed as a choice between bricks and bytes or between books and bytes, and there were even people within the library profession who wondered if the institution of the library would endure when people everywhere could find the information they needed in the brave new world of cyberspace. Was the public library, one of the great social inventions of the nineteenth and twentieth centuries, destined to wither away in the twenty-first?

The publication of *Buildings, Books, and Bytes: Libraries and Communities in the Digital Age* in 1996 focused the controversy within the library community. Commissioned by the Benton Foundation and funded by the W. K. Kellogg Foundation, this book was a report on the public's opinions about the library profession's own vision for the future of the institution. There were many criticisms of the method used to identify both the library leaders who contributed to the profession's library vision and the members of the public who responded to that vision (Goldhor 1997). However, the findings had value in opening up a wider discussion within the library community about the impact of technology on the services libraries could and should provide. The findings also validated the role of children's work as a vital element of public library services. Eighty-three percent of those queried rated services to children as "very important," the highest ranked of all possible roles for the library to play (Benton Foundation 1996, 19).

The findings that proved most troublesome to librarians were warnings about the lack of support by eighteen- to twenty-four-year-olds for maintaining library buildings in a digital environment. In general, the respondents found that libraries were increasingly irrelevant in the digital age. Even readers seemed to prefer the new bookstore chains such as Barnes and Noble and Borders to their local libraries.

The public library profession responded to the challenges outlined in the report and often echoed by local civic decision makers in a variety of ways. One strategy was to increase the role of digitally based information services in public libraries by providing increased access to computers and the Internet. Librarians were portrayed as skilled navigators who could assist ordinary travelers lost on the information superhighway.

Children's librarians were somewhat challenged in their efforts to take this approach by a torrent of opposition from conservative pundits and talk show hosts who claimed that public libraries were exposing children to pornography and other dangers on the Internet. Parents responded in some confusion. In 1999, the *Orange County Register* reported on the range of policies governing public access to the Internet by children and adults at various libraries in Southern California. At that time, these policies ranged from filtering all computers at the Yorba Linda Library to the compromise position of requiring parental permission for unrestricted access for minors in the Orange County library system to completely open access at the Newport Beach Public Library.

Two parents with differing perspectives were interviewed. One father insisted that monitoring his son's computer use was his responsibility, not the library's. He had taught his son rules for safety online and wasn't worried that the ten-year-old boy might stumble onto something unsavory. "These things may happen," the father said. "It just means he has to be given some additional training." On the other hand, a mother was shocked by a librarian's apparent lack of concern when a patron reported that a boy was peeking at a cybersex website. This mother wanted the library to be a safe haven where her daughters could do homework without being exposed to graphic sexual images. She noted that even the local video store kept its X-rated materials off-limits to kids. "What we're asking is for libraries to have the same type of concern for our children — respect for their innocence — that every other establishment seems to have," she said (Chmielewski 1999, 9).

The passage of the Children's Internet Protection Act (CIPA) in 2000 resolved the issue for many public libraries. Under the provisions of this act, public libraries are required to certify that they have an Internet safety policy and technology protection measures in place. They are required to use technological blocks or filters to prevent access to pictures that are obscene, are child pornography, or are harmful to minors on computers that can be used by children. They must adopt and implement policies that address the access by minors to inappropriate matter on the Internet; the security of minors when using electronic mail, chat rooms, and other forms of electronic communication; and the unauthorized disclosure, use, and dissemination of personal information regarding minors. They are even required to take measures to prevent circumvention of the safety measures, or "hacking." Libraries and schools that do not comply are ineligible for funding for Internet access through the discounted E-rate program (Federal Communications Commission 2008). Some libraries have chosen to forgo participation in the E-rate program, but most have apparently decided that filtering children's computers is a compromise with intellectual freedom principles that they can live with.

The American Library Association was a major financial and political partner in the coalition that unsuccessfully fought the adoption of CIPA in the courts. The association maintains a website that provides resources for librarians faced with implementing CIPA and a detailed history of the law and the legal challenges brought against it (ALA n.d.).

Libraries have also tried to position themselves as advocates for those people on the other side of the digital divide, providing access to sophisticated computer technology and digital resources that many still do not have either at home or at work. Library homework centers have been a particularly effective venue for giving young people guidance in using the digital resources in addition to access to word processing programs and other homework tools. I have observed children and their parents getting some basic information literacy instruction from a homework center aide in a Long Beach (California) Public Library branch. Instruction was given informally and naturally in the context of a particular homework assignment. It turns out that having a computer and Internet access in the home does not preclude using those services in the library. Children have told me that they must compete with siblings and parents to use their home computer. Some young people also prefer the more social environment in the library, where, if library rules permit, they can use the computer with a small group of friends rather than in the isolation of their own bedroom.

Computers with high-speed Internet access for public use are now standard equipment in public libraries. They are used by children and teens as well as adults, although most users under the age of 18 will find that their access is somewhat limited by mechanical filtering devices. Recently, public libraries have embraced the principles of Web 2.0, making access to their resources more interactive. It is safe to say that books and bytes now coexist in relative harmony in library buildings and services.

The focus on the library building itself has been an interesting response to the doubts and questions raised in the 1990s. Even while some prophets within and outside the profession were predicting the demise of the bricks-and-mortar library in favor of the electronic "library without walls," some public libraries were redefining themselves as "destination places." These libraries were designed as places where people would choose to go and spend some time, not just pick up a book or check their e-mail. The children's spaces in these newly conceptualized public libraries often received special attention.

The Cerritos Millennium Library, dedicated in 2002, was one of the first libraries to receive national attention for its intentional use of architectural and design elements to create a unique user experience. Its website explains that the library was inspired in part by the book *The Experience Economy* by B. Joseph Pine and James H. Gilmore, a Harvard Business School Press publication of 1999. The key concepts underlying the design are

- redefining the library user as "end product"
- championing The Book while integrating electronic resources
- engineering the physical environment to create dynamic, multimedia learning opportunities
- extending customer/public service in a more proactive way (www.ci.cerritos.ca.us/library/fact_sheet.html)

The library is the centerpiece of a redesigned civic center in this suburban Southern California city. The interior of the library is designed as a series of themed spaces, including an Old World reading room with wood paneling and a Gothic fireplace complete with holographic flames, an Art Deco teen space, and, of course, the children's room, which may be the library's most notable area.

The Cerritos Library's children's room has a saltwater aquarium, a lighthouse in which children can curl up and read, a model space shuttle, and a full-sized replica of a *Tyrannosaurus rex* fossil. A simulated rain forest canopy covers part of the reading room. The area has a craft room, a story theater, and many interactive learning stations. The room has low ambient lighting with strategic track lighting over the ample book stacks and banks of computer terminals. On a recent summer Saturday morning, many families were visiting this stimulating space. They all seemed quietly engaged with its resources—browsing the stacks, reading together in the many comfortable areas designed for this purpose, watching the sharks in the fish tank, using the computers. Interestingly, there was little obvious staff presence. A young man behind the help desk was friendly and responded when approached, but there were no librarians or other employees interacting with the "end products" out on the spacious floor. Perhaps during the school year there is more need for reference assistance, but on this occasion patrons were managing the experience on their own.

ImaginOn: The Joe and Joan Martin Center in Charlotte, North Carolina, bills itself on its website as "an exciting destination for families, a place where journeys of imagination begin and stories come to life" (www .imaginon.org). A joint venture between the Public Library of Charlotte and Mecklenburg County (PLCMC) and the Children's Theatre of Charlotte, this exuberant facility aims to be "the first place that families and their children think of when they want to spend quality time together." Located just a few blocks from the library system's central library, this 102,000-square-foot building provides ample opportunities for interactive experiences. The theater and the library each occupies its own space while sharing the Story Lab in the middle of the ground floor. In the Story Lab, children can create their own stories at whimsical computer stations, act them out in costume on a stage with a closed-circuit television camera, or put on a puppet show. Children can play in a stationary trolley and marvel at the huge Story Jar representing all the stories in the world.

A ramp leads to the second floor, devoted to classrooms, computers, a Teen Loft, and a studio where young people can produce live-action and animated videos. Even the more traditional library for younger children on the first floor is filled with design elements that invite the child's active participation. There are magnet boards on the ends of stacks and an inviting dollhouse, children's art on the bulletin board walls, and a child-sized information desk.

Because of the center's location in a downtown area with few nearby residences, children are not likely to come to ImaginOn alone—although teens do seem to use public transportation to get there on their own. The building is geared for class visits, with parking spaces for buses and designated indoor and outdoor locations for classes to eat their lunches. There is a sign-in desk in the lobby for groups. On the Saturday that I visited, a volunteer greeted each person at the entrance and offered assistance in orienting each visitor to the stimulating environment.

The Cerritos Library and ImaginOn represent extreme—and costly—examples of public libraries' efforts to make their buildings inviting destinations. They put the lie to the fear expressed in the 1990s that the era of bricks-and-mortar libraries was over. They also validate the notion that public libraries occupy a very special place in the lives of children and families. Not every community has the resources to make such a massive investment, of course. More modest efforts are being made in many libraries to reinvent themselves as essential community spaces.

A new focus on early-childhood services has been a stimulus for some of the changes in library facilities. Developmentally appropriate practice has suggested some modifications to traditional children's rooms. Babies and their caregivers, for example, need soft, padded floor coverings and smooth edges on shelves and seating. A literacy-rich environment for two-year-olds would include three-dimensional letters to manipulate in addition to books. When Michigan's West Bloomfield Township Public Library redesigned its children's area to attract families to spend more time there, the plans included a baby crawl space where infants could safely explore while their mothers or caregivers kept watch. The librarian in charge of the teen and children's areas of the new Burton Barr Central Library in Phoenix, Arizona, carved an early-learning space out of the children's reading room. Its low benches make comfortable seating for adult caregivers, while the soft, rubbery floor is safe for infants. Staff members here are constantly looking for new ways to attract families to stay and engage in activities that foster emergent literacy skills. Library administrators in West Bloomfield Township and Phoenix point out that extreme weather conditions in their communities—cold in Michigan and heat in Arizona—also contribute to the desirability of positioning the library as a climate-controlled indoor haven for families and caregivers of young children.

Family Place (www.familyplacelibraries.org) is an initiative begun at the Middle Country Public Library in New York in partnership with the nonprofit organization Libraries for the Future. It has expanded to include more than 220 sites in twenty-three states. Family Place Libraries redesign their physical facility to be welcoming and appropriate for very young children and their families. These spaces offer a core collection of books, toys, music, and multimedia materials and serve as the venues for parent-child workshops in which professionals from a variety of fields share skills and knowledge that contribute to the healthy development of young children.

What would William Fletcher think of a contemporary public library children's room with its soft floor coverings, low picture book shelving, rows of computer stations, and baskets of manipulatives for young children to play with? Public libraries have changed and so have the librarians who work in them. No longer judgmental keepers of culture, librarians who specialize in service for children have expanded their notions of good practice to meet new expectations and challenges. In the next chapter, we will examine the contemporary implications of the century-old tradition of library service to the children in the United States.

TWO

The Legacy Reconsidered

WE CAN SEE FROM THE NARRATIVE IN CHAPTER 1 THAT LIBRARY SERVICE to children has a long and rich tradition in the United States. Children's librarians today are linked through this history to the foremothers who opened the doors to children at the turn of the twentieth century and to the librarians of the 1960s and 1970s who went outside the doors of their libraries to reach the children who hadn't yet found the library building. We share a history with those librarians who dared to make the children's rooms in their Carnegie libraries less orderly and efficient and more child-friendly. We celebrate the organizational skills of the librarians who successfully institutionalized the Newbery and Caldecott Medals awarded to distinguished books for children and those who demonstrated the tangible results of their work through output measures. We owe a great deal to all those advocates for children and libraries who came before us.

In this chapter, we will turn a more analytical eye on the legacy that is both a gift and a burden to those of us who care about getting it right for children and libraries.

I propose that six principles of library service to children were established in the early years and have remained constant with some adaptations for over a hundred years. They represent our core values. Together, these six principles form the foundation on which the service and the profession have been built:

- Reading good books contributes to a good life.
- Readers' advisory services, storytelling, and booktalks are the key strategies for promoting reading.
- The individual child is the primary user of children's library service.
- The library's children's room is an integral element in library service to children.

- Children's librarians are the appropriate specialists who can best deliver library service to children.
- Children's librarians are advocates for library service to children.

In addition to these six founding principles, two themes have emerged more recently:

- Libraries provide children with information as well as pleasure reading.
- Library service to children can be optimized through partnerships and collaborations.

Finally, two themes have waxed and waned over the years as social conditions and perceptions of the role of the library have changed:

- Library use is a civic activity.
- Americans and American libraries have a responsibility to look beyond their borders and to adopt a global perspective.

In this chapter, we will look at the original principles with an eye to seeing how each holds up at the end of the first decade of the twenty-first century. In the next chapter, we will turn to the second and third sets of themes that are more recent in their manifestations.

The Six Core Values

1. Reading good books contributes to a good life.

The founding mothers of children's library services were passionate believers in the power of reading to shape an individual child's character. In chapter 1, we learned that these women were products of the Progressive Era who shared with other well-meaning and well-educated people of their time an optimistic belief in the perfectability of human beings and the constant improvement of society. Those librarians who were creating library service to children at the beginning of the twentieth century were committed to providing children with books to read not because reading was fun but because reading was essential to their intellectual, aesthetic, and moral development.

Although finding pleasure in reading was only a secondary consideration, librarians wisely shunned the dull, preachy tracts that formed much of the literature published for children at that time. They soon developed standards for quality in children's literature that distinguished between the didacticism of the Sunday school publications on the one hand and the trashy dime novels and pulp literature that formed much of the popular reading on the other. They were looking for books that were more entertaining than the former and more substantial than the latter.

It is significant that the 1929 yearbook of children's library services devoted most of its content to children's books. Those Jazz Age children's librarians prided themselves on their knowledge of good children's literature. They also took responsibility for sharing that knowledge, thereby promoting good reading for boys and girls.

It was no accident, then, that the fields of children's book publishing and children's librarianship developed in parallel. Public libraries were a major market for children's books, and librarians like Anne Carroll Moore, strategically located in New York, were not shy about trying to influence publishers, authors, and illustrators to produce the kinds of books they wanted to share with children. Moore, for example, wrote one of the earliest columns in a general periodical devoted to reviews of children's books. She also cultivated relationships with prominent authors and illustrators, offering often unsolicited advice. Her unfavorable response to E. B. White's *Stuart Little* has become the stuff of legend in the library and literary communities, and recently, thanks to an article in *The New Yorker*, more broadly known to the reading public (Lepore 2008).

The children's library establishment occasionally clashed with the progressive education community. Both Anne Carroll Moore and Frances Clarke Sayers, her successor at New York Public Library, were outspoken in their disdain for the "here-and-now" realism espoused by the faculty at the influential Bank Street School. In her 1937 speech "Lose Not the Nightingale," Sayers criticized the currently fashionable theories of modern education as robbing reading of its challenge to the mind and the imagination of the child. She worried that education's emphasis on practical experience limited the child's ability to respond to the intuitive and the poetic. She also railed against the insistence of the education community on measuring reading ability and defining what words children should know at a certain age. She criticized teachers and librarians who "look at books as though they were pieces of merchandise, scanning the page for words—not ideas—and condemning them upon that basis. They read with no open ears to hear what revelation the writer may have to make, what bit of originality he may have created; what heights of feeling, what humorous point of view he may be seeking to share" (1965, 61).

Certainly books and reading are still at the heart of library service to children. The Association for Library Service to Children (ALSC) still proudly announces the winners of the Newbery and Caldecott Medals to an audience of thousands at ALA's annual conference. It has even added to the categories of books to be honored: the Sibert Medal for informational books, the Geisel Medal for independent readers, the Batchelder Award for a book in translation. The Laura Ingalls Wilder Award is given every other year to an author or illustrator honored for a body of work. ALSC has partnered with REFORMA, the National Association to Promote Library and Information Services to Latinos and the Spanish Speaking, to create the Pura Belpré Medal given to Latino authors and illustrators of distinguished books for children, and it continues to promote the Coretta Scott King Book Awards given to African American authors and illustrators.

Many members of ALSC feel that serving on a committee to select the Newbery or Caldecott Medal winners is the pinnacle of their careers. A proposal in 2008 for a bylaws change in the way that the chairpersons of these committees would be selected generated an unusual amount of heated debate on the association's electronic discussion list. However, even more controversy and heat were generated by Anita Silvey when she suggested in a *School Library Journal* article that the Newbery Medal may have lost its luster. She quoted a number of anonymous sources in the library and children's literature communities who claimed to have been disappointed with recent choices that lacked child appeal. She writes, "Booksellers told me that selling a Newbery winner during the 1990s was as easy as picking an apple off a tree, because the choices usually excited them. But 'in the past few years,' explained one veteran, 'we haven't sold a single copy of the Newbery'" (Silvey 2008). Silvey speculated that the committee members responsible for selecting the award winner have been led astray by uniqueness and quirkiness, abandoning the classic criteria for the best children's book of the year.

It is possible that children's librarians' traditional affiliation with the cause of good books for children is no longer a source of strength and distinction. Even within the profession, there are fewer among us who maintain book collections based on the standards of quality espoused by earlier librarians. Few librarians would admit to collecting nothing but trash, but most would confess to catering more and more to popular taste.

Although earlier librarians refused to stock popular series books such as Nancy Drew and the Hardy Boys, contemporary librarians buy multiple copies of whatever series attracts young readers today. In fact, attracting young readers has become the primary goal for most library children's departments. Certainly there are still librarians who are effective at hand selling the good stuff, one book and one child at a time, adhering to the old mantra, "the right book for the right child." There are still librarians who assiduously booktalk the finest books in their collections, sparking a run on titles such as Nancy Farmer's *The Ear, the Eye, and the Arm*, Virginia Hamilton's *Planet of Junior Brown*, or Jennifer Roy's *Yellow Star*, often on the basis of their personal credibility and infectious enthusiasm alone. There are still librarians who convince classroom teachers and parents to read aloud some of the great books that might be just a little beyond the reading level of the children in their charge.

However, it is more common to find children's librarians using bait-and-switch marketing techniques — luring kids to the library with promises of stacks of Junie B. Jones and Captain Underpants books while hanging on to the hope that once they've crossed the threshold they can be enticed to try something a little meatier. Another justification offered by librarians who stock their collections with a wide assortment of more popular titles is that children have the same right to light reading as adults do. Just as libraries stock best-selling titles of dubious literary merit because that is what taxpaying adult patrons want, so should libraries give children what they want. Of course, what children want is often the result of massive marketing campaigns by adults with commercial interests at stake. However, both the bait-and-switch approach and the children's rights argument can be seen as reasoned choices made by librarians who have thought about children and books. I have less sympathy for a response I have heard from some librarians around the country when I ask them what kids are reading in their communities. Sometimes they whisper. Sometimes they whine. The tone may vary, but the content is the same: "Kids don't read as much as they used to." "Reading scores are down." "All they want to do is play on the computer." "Teachers don't push reading anymore." "The job isn't as much fun as it used to be." These librarians have just given up.

It is true that nationally children's reading scores are down from previous years. There is some evidence that children are spending more time in front of screens than ever before, whether they are playing video games, using the Internet for a variety of reasons, or watching television. Many children's lives are scheduled down to the minute, leaving little time for voluntary pleasure reading. Twenty-first-century librarians who have not given up are responding by moving aggressively into the early literacy business as they try to ensure that children at least have the right foundation for the complex set of skills that are involved in reading.

There are a number of national library-based early learning initiatives, each of which makes the development of emergent literacy skills its primary goal. I will discuss one of these programs, Family Place, a little later in this chapter as a current response to creating appropriate spaces in libraries for children. The initiative that has early literacy most clearly at its core is "Every Child Ready to Read @ your library" (ECRR).

ECRR is the result of a partnership between two divisions of the American Library Association—the Association for Library Service to Children (ALSC) and the Public Library Association (PLA). ECRR is a research-based program designed to help parents and caregivers give the infants, toddlers, and preschoolers in their care the essential skills they need to be ready and eager to learn to read when they start their formal schooling. Librarians are trained to conduct three different workshops in which the parents and caregivers learn the six essential literacy skills that children must master *before* they formally learn to read and, more important, how they can help children acquire those skills. The six essential preliteracy skills that the program emphasizes are

- vocabulary
- print motivation
- print awareness
- narrative skills
- letter knowledge
- phonological awareness

The assumption is that these skills need constant reinforcement during a child's first four years of life. Even a weekly visit to the library for storytime would not provide the kind of sustained contact needed to inculcate the knowledge and skills represented. Librarians, therefore, enlist the parents and caregivers, who have daily contact with young children, as the primary teachers of these foundational skills.

So far this has been a discussion of the ways in which twenty-first-century librarians think about reading. Most of us became librarians because we are lifelong readers ourselves. We have found both pleasure and knowledge in books; we know how reading can enrich lives. We want to share that richness with children. At our best, we develop book collections that reflect the reading needs and interests of the children in our communities. We use creative, sensitive strategies to introduce children to good books that they might not think to pick up on their own, often expanding their understanding of the world and their places in it. We take books outside our walls to children who can't come to us. We stock our shelves with books in languages other than English so that children who are newcomers to this country will still be able to read and be read to. We have replaced the traditional mantra of "the right book for the right child" with an expanded version: "the right book for the right child at the right time at the right place." We enlist parents, caregivers, and other community partners in initiatives that support the development of a child's literacy skills. Let us look next at the traditional ways in which we continue to promote books and reading: booktalks, storytelling, and readers' advisory services.

2. Readers' advisory services, storytelling, and booktalks are the key strategies for promoting reading.

No national statistics are available to document the amount of booktalking, storytelling, and readers' advisory services being practiced by children's librarians, now or in the past. We must rely on anecdotal evidence and observation here. The founding mothers introduced storytelling as a way to foster an appreciation for language and for traditional folktales. Anne Pellowski (1990) reports that storytelling programs seem to have begun spontaneously at the Carnegie Library in Pittsburgh and the Pratt Institute Free Library in Brooklyn at about the same time in 1899. Mary Wright Plummer is usually credited with introducing storytelling to children at the Pratt Institute. Her inspiration was Marie Shedlock, a British storyteller who presented a program of Hans Christian Andersen tales to an adult audience at Sherry's Ballroom in New York City. Shedlock was invited to tell stories at Pratt in 1906, where Anna Cogswell Tyler, then a library school student, was in the audience. Two years later, Anne Carroll Moore invited Tyler to be the head of storytelling for New York Public Library (NYPL), thus institutionalizing the practice. Interestingly, there is no evidence that Moore herself ever told stories, but she made the traditional art of oral storytelling an integral part of library service to children. By 1900, at least five other public libraries had begun offering story hours, and the practice spread widely as graduates of the Carnegie and Pratt training programs were hired elsewhere (Pellowski 1990, 98).

Generations of children's librarians at NYPL were trained in that traditional style of storytelling. I was trained in the NYPL approach by Mae Durham when I was in library school at the University of California, Berkeley. We were taught to avoid overly dramatic gestures and gimmicky props or costumes as being distractions from the purity of the story itself. We didn't memorize the story unless it was an original tale, such as one of Carl Sandberg's *Rootabaga Stories*. Rather, we learned the outline of the story, its mood and tone, perhaps memorizing a distinctive opening or closing and a few essential phrases or refrains. The trick was to channel the story and let one's own personality fade into the background. Over the years, I adapted my own storytelling style to include some of those forbidden gestures and props and allowed myself to emote more than Mae Durham would have approved. I still honor the basic precept though: it's all about the story, not the teller.

Children's librarians were expected to hold regular story hours for school-age children at my first two library jobs, in Sunnyvale and San Francisco, California. We used the traditional ritual of lighting a candle to start the program, blowing it out with a wish to mark the close. My experience was that the audience was small but loyal, entranced by the ritual of the wishing candle as well as the stories themselves. Far more children heard folktales during the visits that we made to schools or that classes made to the library. It was our practice to invite every third-grade class to visit the library and to visit every fourth-grade class in our service area. We told a story on each occasion. To this day, I can tell "The Hobyahs" and "The Little Rooster, the Turkish Sultan, and the Diamond Button" at the drop of a hat, having told them dozens, if not hundreds, of times to schoolchildren back in the late 1960s.

There is little evidence that regular story hours are conducted in many public libraries today. The "Competencies for Librarians Serving Children in Public Libraries," adopted by ALSC in 1999, simply include storytelling as one of many options under "Programming Skills." Storytelling is still a popular course at UCLA where I teach, but it is not even offered at many graduate programs of library and information studies. Children's librarians who have learned the craft of storytelling and who enjoy sharing stories with older children tend to tell one story at a time to groups of children, as we did with school and class visits back in the 1960s, or as a segment in a program that may also include a puppet show, a craft demonstration, a magician, or a video showing.

Storytelling for preschool children, on the other hand, has become a ubiquitous part of library programming. This event has expanded from the traditional preschool storytime for three- and four-year-olds to specialized programming for toddlers, infants, and family groups. These programs include picture-book and flannelboard stories, fingerplays, songs, nursery rhymes, and lots and lots of audience participation.

Booktalking has taken its place with preschool storytimes as a staple of most children's librarians' toolkits. Michael Sullivan (2005) defines it as standing up in front of a group of people and telling them why they would want to read a book. He defines and gives examples of six different types of booktalks: plot summary, character sketch, vignette, dialogue, theme, and media tie-in. It would be unusual to base an entire program on booktalks, although I have occasionally been asked to do this for adult audiences looking for ideas for gift books during the winter holidays, multicultural books to share with elementary school children, or good books for school principals to read aloud. More typically, a children's librarian will include a few booktalks when addressing a school class. These presentations might highlight new books in the library or books related to a current assignment. Sometimes librarians use booktalks of popular titles in order to lure kids into the library: "Look, if you want Captain Underpants books, we've got 'em!"

Librarians also booktalk titles while working on the floor of the library, hand selling individual books to individual patrons. This individualized promotion of books is an essential component of readers' advisory service and is more appropriately addressed in our discussion of the next core value: service to the individual child. In fact, when we think about connecting children with books, we usually think about an individual child who is standing in front of us in the children's room. "This will be a great book to share with Julio; he is crazy about robots." "I've got to remember to give this book about frogs to Joey at storytime next week." "I wish this book had been on the shelf last week when Tanesha was asking for a book about sisters who fight." Let us take a little time to think about the tradition of serving the individual child and its implications for twenty-first-century library service.

3. The individual child is the primary user of children's library service.

Librarians often talk about the "regulars," the boys and girls who are in the library nearly every day after school. Some of these are avid readers whom we struggle to supply with enough books to feed their habit. Others are latchkey kids who use the library as de facto after-school child care, usually by parental design. Although some of these latchkey children are also readers who find the library the perfect place to spend a couple of hours waiting for their parents to pick them up, others seem to be restless prisoners confined in a place that is too small and too quiet.

Creative, concerned librarians look for ways to make the library a welcoming place for those children who have not chosen to be there. Computers, homework centers, and after-school activities have helped to occupy the children's time in productive ways. Still, when latchkey children are the dominant library users in that three to six o'clock afternoon period, they are rarely seen as individuals. They are often perceived by library staff as an undifferentiated mass, and not always a desirable one.

In some communities, however, the problem is a different one. Children may find geographic or social barriers to getting to the library on their own. The library may be too far away for the child to walk or ride a bike. Public transportation may be inadequate. The route to the library may be perceived as too dangerous because of traffic or street crime. Children in these circumstances are usually dependent on their parents to take them to the library. In some cases, the parent simply stops at the library on the way home from work and picks up books for her or his children. In these cases, of course, the librarian doesn't even see the child. A classic situation that librarians talk about is dealing with the pushy parent who doesn't let the child speak or select the book that he or she really wants: "That's too easy, Madison; pick something at your grade level." Melissa Gross has also called our attention to the case of the parent acting on behalf of the absent child with a homework assignment in her model of the imposed query, calling this situation the "double imposed query." These reference questions do not originate with the child. First, a teacher has posed the assignment for the child. Then the parent has taken on the responsibility of finding the proper resources for the child's assignment (Gross 2006). Is it any wonder that the original question or homework task often gets garbled, much like the message in the old party game of "telephone"?

Increasingly, the librarian interacts with children in groups, with classes visiting the library or in the classroom itself and with audiences of children attending storytimes and other programs. More and more, librarians find themselves acting as performers or public speakers, a surprise for some of the more introverted recruits to the profession.

There is no evidence that the founding librarians anticipated another change in the service population of library services to children. Children's librarians are serving parents, child care providers, and other adults who work with children in a variety of new ways. As noted in the previous section, children's librarians have joined the national effort to combat illiteracy by reaching out to parents and caregivers. A key component in library early literacy initiatives is educating those adults in techniques and strategies for nurturing emergent literacy skills and knowledge in children from birth to age 4 or 5, before they begin their formal schooling. So children's librarians have taken on yet another role, as adult educators. For many children's librarians, this shift has meant acquiring a new knowledge base—early child development and emergent literacy—and a new skill set—teaching methods.

In the early days of library service to children, the individual child who was being served was ordinarily of school age, between 6 and 14. Preschool children were not considered old enough to use the library collections nor were there appropriate books for them. Adolescence had not yet been invented, so young people over the age of 14 used the adult collection. So another significant change in our thinking has been a steady lowering of the age of the child for whom we provide our service.

The presence of very young children in our public libraries has also given rise to a new emphasis on "developmentally appropriate practice" as it is understood in the early childhood education community (Copple and Bredekamp 2009). Specialists in early childhood education have codified the ways in which adults can most effectively and appropriately interact with children under the age of 8. The "Every Child Ready to Read" program cited earlier is based on principles of developmentally appropriate practice as well as research about early childhood literacy.

The physical space in which we provide library service to children has retained its importance in our overall service delivery system, but like the original focus on the individual child, it has evolved in many ways in response to changes in our understanding of the children we serve and the ways in which we serve them. We will look at some of those changes next.

4. The library's children's room is an integral element in library service to children.

From the beginning, the library children's room was intended to send a clear message to children: this is your place. Follow our simple rules for good behavior, and you will be welcome here. How was this message communicated? By child-sized furniture and low shelving. By books that were meant to please a school-age child. And perhaps most important, by the presence of a friendly young woman who knew your name and the kinds of books you liked to read.

Librarians still aim to make the children's area attractive and welcoming. Styles change, of course, and the dark wood, fresh flower bouquets, and fireplaces of the early libraries have been replaced in many places by bright plastic chairs, "Read" posters, and computer stations. More significant, however, are three trends that are changing the way we think about library space for children. These trends are homework centers, renewed emphasis on early literacy, and the library as "destination place."

Public library service to children was not originally intended as a supplement to schooling. In fact, at various times during its evolution, library policy makers made a conscious effort to differentiate public library services from those offered by school libraries. The conventional wisdom in California during the 1960s, for example, was that public libraries could not afford to provide supplementary school texts or to stock materials that primarily met children's homework needs. Furthermore, it was argued that funding for school libraries, already threatened in the state, might be cut even farther if the public library took up the slack. As it happened, elementary school libraries lost their funding anyway, and most public libraries found themselves unable to ignore the school-related information needs of their young patrons.

Cindy Mediavilla (2001) has pointed out some additional stimuli for the advent of formal homework assistance programs in public libraries. One was the presence of large numbers of latchkey children who invaded many libraries after school. A second phenomenon was the difficulty faced by working parents or by parents who didn't speak English when it came to helping their children with their homework. When the California State Library sponsored a statewide initiative to find out what low-income and racially diverse people wanted from their public libraries, it discovered that overwhelmingly what parents wanted was support for their children's educational success.

Similar findings across the United States resulted in the implementation of homework centers in many public libraries, affecting the physical facility as well as the services offered there. These homework centers were sometimes as modest as a dedicated table where a volunteer tutor would work with individual children. Other libraries found ways to convert little-used meeting rooms or magazine storage rooms into well-equipped spaces with computer stations, reference books, and tables where tutors work with children. Some branch libraries declared the entire public space to be a homework center from three to five o'clock.

If school-age children dominate many public libraries during the after-school hours, it is the preschool children and their caregivers who take over during the mornings and early afternoons—and sometimes early evenings as well. As noted earlier, public libraries have gotten into the early childhood literacy business in a big way. The requirement for "developmentally appropriate practice" affects the design of the physical facility as well as the kinds of services offered.

The authors of *Learning Environments for Young Children* (Feinberg, Kuchner, and Feldman 1998) remind librarians that anything that can be moved, turned, poked, or manipulated by a young child will be. Heating units and electrical sockets must be covered or out of reach. Furniture must have rounded edges. Children must have room to move freely and to express themselves at a noise level that is above the traditional library whisper. Parents and caregivers must be accommodated as well; not every adult is comfortable getting down on the rug with the children. I like the curved bench in the early childhood area at the Burton Barr Central Library in Phoenix, Arizona. It serves as a room divider, houses picture books in the space below the seating, and makes it possible for adults to stay comfortably close to their children.

Libraries that have joined the Family Place Libraries (www.family placelibraries.org) movement provide a "specially designed, welcoming space" in addition to a collection of books, music, and toys and programming based on parent-child workshops. These spaces look much like preschool classrooms with their blocks and toys. The parent-child workshops are designed to teach parenting skills in a natural, nonthreatening environment. These Family Place spaces can take up a lot of floor space; smaller libraries sometimes store the special equipment in a closet and bring it out only for the regularly scheduled workshops.

In the first chapter, I talked about some of the libraries that had transformed themselves into destination places, where patrons of all ages would be drawn to visit and spend time. One new library destination place combines the focus on emergent literacy with an alluring space designed specifically for children from birth to age 5 and their caregivers. Storyville, located at the Rosedale branch of the Baltimore County Public Library, is a 2,240-square-foot, child-sized village with seven different learning areas: a library, a house, a theater, a store, a Chesapeake Bay waterfront, a baby garden, and a construction site. Each area is furnished with books and interactive materials that generate activities that promote language and literacy and other school readiness skills. It must be very, very popular. According to the "frequently asked questions" on the Storyville website, the waiting time to enter Storyville can be as long as an hour (www.bcpl storyville.org/storyville_about.html). The pictures on Storyville's website show children in a variety of interactive settings that would not be out of place in a good children's museum. Mary Wright Plummer and her contemporaries would be amazed.

5. Children's librarians are the appropriate specialists who can best deliver library service to children.

Anne Carroll Moore and the other founding mothers had to invent the specialization of children's librarianship. Moore's recognition of the importance of this specialization is reflected in the "Four Respects" she formulated while at New York Public Library:

> First, respect for the children.
>
> Second, respect for the books.
>
> Third, respect for the children's librarian as an integral element in the library's organization.
>
> Fourth, and finally, respect for the professional status of children's librarianship. (Cummins 1999)

In the first chapter we learned how early administrators recruited and trained the first cohorts of women to be children's librarians. (Men entered this branch of the profession much later.) Christine Jenkins has described the role as defined in those days as being a kind of "friendly and unsentimental older sister" (Hearne and Jenkins 1999). This friendly big sister almost certainly saw her major role as providing the children who came to her library with good, wholesome books to read.

The big sisters (and brothers, too) who now staff public libraries' children's rooms probably still see their primary function as providing children with good books to read. As noted earlier in this chapter, they may no longer agree that those books must be either "good" as defined by some literary criteria or wholesome. It may be enough just to get children reading anything. However, the duties of a children's librarian have expanded far beyond the collection development and readers' advisory responsibilities that were the core tasks of a librarian one hundred years ago.

The ALSC "Competencies for Librarians Serving Children in Public Libraries" (1999) divide the sphere of work into seven categories: knowledge of client group; administrative and management skills; communication skills; materials and collection development; programming skills; advocacy, public relations, and networking skills; and professionalism and professional development. My UCLA students think that technology and training skills, though perhaps inferred in several of these categories, should be added to the list. It is a formidable array of skills and knowledge to master, and yet children's librarians manage to do it.

Most children's librarians acquire the foundations on which to continue to hone their skills during their period of study in a graduate program of library and information science. At UCLA, we encourage students to think about their ongoing plan for continuing education even before they graduate, reminding them that our field is unusually dynamic. These dedicated children's librarians see their work as a highly specialized branch of librarianship, requiring particular kinds of preparation. However, as graduate library schools—or information schools, as many now call themselves—cut back on their course work in the area of children's and young adult services, many libraries must hire people without that specialized training. Larger systems may have staff who can make up for the lack of skills and knowledge through special training programs. Other libraries may find themselves in the position of hiring generalists or even people who trained to be adult reference librarians or catalogers.

It often seems like too much to expect any one person to do—planning and implementing a broad range of services for children from birth to age 12 or 14. Large libraries with ample resources sometimes divide the work, with a specialist for preschool services or relationships with schools, for example. This is still unusual, however, and most children's librarians find ways to juggle it all. Role strain and burnout are the negative consequences for some.

However, a survey conducted by *School Library Journal* (Kenney 2009) shows that most children's librarians are satisfied with their jobs. The three top sources of satisfaction for children's librarians working in public libraries are working with young people, assisting customers, and connecting kids to reading and lifelong learning. The most common areas of dissatisfaction are inadequate library funding, low salary, and increased workload. The median salary for children's librarians working in public libraries was reported as $37,500 compared with $62,500 for a teacher-librarian.

In his article reporting on the job satisfaction survey, Kenney (2009, 31) notes the need to recruit more young and more diverse people to the profession. It is encouraging, therefore, that 93 percent of the survey respondents reported that they would recommend the field enthusiastically or with some reservations. And 93 percent said that they would do it all over again if they were starting now to choose their careers.

6. Children's librarians are advocates for library service to children.

Mary Wright Plummer, Anne Carroll Moore, and those other women who invented library service to children more than one hundred years ago were unusually effective advocates for children. They represented the rights of children both within their own library organizations and in the national professional associations. They fought for dedicated space in libraries and for circulation policies and fee structures that were child-friendly. They fought to make children's rooms comfortable and welcoming places at a time when Carnegie's building planners were trying to dictate a much colder and more formal environment. They fought for respect for the children and for the specialization of children's librarianship.

Most children's librarians still see themselves as advocates for children and for library services for children. Their primary target for advocacy efforts is probably their own library. It is hoped the whining that they were so often accused of in the past has been replaced by effective, current management practices. More and more children's librarians, for example, are making use of techniques such as outcome-based planning and evaluation (to be discussed at much more length in chapter 5) to justify the impact of their work.

Advocacy does not stop at the library's door, however. The sixth competency for librarians serving children in public libraries is "advocacy, public relations, and networking skills" (ALSC 1999). This competency encompasses a variety of skills intended to promote awareness and support for children's interests in the broader community as well as within the library itself. Looking at the nine bullet points listed under this competency heading, we get a picture of the children's librarian as a dynamic player in organizational and political arenas. Most children's librarians do their most effective advocacy through organizations such as state and national professional associations that have professional lobbyists on staff.

Advocating for children's intellectual freedom is a major responsibility for children's librarians and one that often results in tensions and conflicts for individuals. Some children's librarians have told me that they feel uncomfortable with their own library's policy to filter computers used by young patrons. They are daunted by the prospect of trying to change a policy that has been set by powerful political decision makers and presumably accepted by the library's administration, but they know that the best interests of the child are not being served.

I recently met with a small working group of librarians who were putting together a panel presentation on children's rights to be presented at the fiftieth anniversary of the MLIS program at UCLA. Group members expressed diverse opinions about the common policy and practice in public libraries to defer to parents who choose to limit their own children's access to certain books or media. All of us acknowledged the practicality of such a policy; it lets the library off the hook in many a potentially explosive situation. Letting parents decide the parameters for their own child and only their own child makes it possible to keep some controversial materials on the shelf. However, some of us worried about the rights of the child whose parents had not let him check out a Harry Potter book because its depiction of wizards and witchcraft conflicted with the family's religious beliefs. Do we have any responsibility to advocate for the child's intellectual freedom in that situation? One of our group argued that if the child really wanted it and knew we had it, he'd figure out how to get it. I am not so sure, but I don't have a practical solution to this dilemma. We will talk more about this issue in chapter 4.

Children's librarians have still not won the salaries that would be commensurate with the requirements of their jobs. We noted earlier that children's librarians in public libraries make much less than teacher-librarians do, and they still rank lower than reference librarians. A search on a national job salary database (www.indeed.com) showed the average salary for children's librarians in California to be $46,000; for reference librarians in the state, the average salary is $48,000. It is true that children's librarians' job satisfaction is usually high in spite of the lack of monetary reward, but it would be very nice if they—or someone else—advocated on their behalf for a change.

Looking back at all of the six core values of our profession that have persisted to this day, we can say that they are still valid. They still inform the work we do and provide us with continuity and stability. These values or principles have provided a consistent base from which we have been able to evolve as the needs of children and the world they live in have changed. In the next chapter, we will continue our reconsideration of the legacy by looking at two values that have emerged more recently and at two others that have waxed and waned in importance or relevance over the years.

THREE

Emerging Issues

WE HAVE LOOKED AT THE SIX CORE VALUES THAT HAVE BEEN TRANS-mitted to twenty-first-century children's librarians through the chain of men and women who came before us, going back at least a hundred years. We have noted the ways in which some of those values have evolved or have been reinterpreted for new generations of children in new circumstances. In this chapter, we will continue to reconsider our legacy, turning first to two values or principles that have emerged more recently in our history:

- Libraries provide children with information as well as pleasure reading.
- Library service to children can be optimized through partnerships and collaborations.

The Information Role of Library Service to Children

The founding mothers didn't write much about the library as a source of information for children. There is not even much mention of "reference services" in the early canon of writing about library service for children. The term *reference* does not appear in either the index or the table of contents of Barbara T. Rollock's *Public Library Services for Children* (1988). A chapter on "the multifaceted services of the children's department" is concerned almost entirely with programming—storytelling, booktalking, films, and so on.

By the 1990s, however, manuals and guides for children's librarians included reference as a significant aspect of the work. Rosemarie Riechel (1991) devoted a whole book to the subject. Jane Gardner

Connor went so far as to claim that reference and readers' advisory services are the major responsibilities of librarians working with children (1990, 52). My own assessment of children's librarianship in 2001 was that increased homework-related queries and the ubiquity of digital resources were changing the landscape of reference services for kids (Walter 2001, 29–32). Michael Sullivan's 2005 book on children's library service devotes an entire chapter to the topic. He opens that chapter, however, with the statement that "reference work is most often associated with adult services" (88) even as he points out that children ask more questions per capita than adults do, according to data from the Public Library Data Service's *Statistical Report '97* (PLA 1997).

We could speculate about reasons for the increased attention to reference work as an aspect of library service to children. In California, at least, the lack of libraries in elementary schools means that children must use the public library to meet their homework-related information needs. Our collections may be more attuned to those information needs, and our public access computers with Internet connections are attractive resources for many children.

In any case, the burgeoning scholarly research on information-seeking behavior provides a useful framework for thinking about how we can best design and implement effective reference services for children.

When I did my research on the information needs of ten-year-olds in the early 1990s (Walter 1994), there was nothing else in the research or professional literature that looked specifically at children as information seekers. I learned in that preliminary work that adults who interacted with children in a variety of ways—teachers, ministers, soccer coaches, day-care providers, nurses, librarians—observed a host of information needs that mapped with remarkable consistency to Abraham Maslow's hierarchy of needs. Equally remarkable was the lack of information providers who could help most children meet those information needs. Even librarians did not see it as part of their mission, for example, to help children learn to be wise consumers or to be more aware of their own emotional states, although these were areas about which adult professionals found that children lacked information.

Subsequent research helped us understand those information needs that were not generated by the child but rather by some external agent, such as a teacher. These "imposed queries" require a particular kind of reference interview in order to ferret out what the child's needs really are (Gross 2006). Ya-Ling Lu did her doctoral research on ways in which librarians handle parents' requests for materials that will help their young children adjust to big and little changes and upsets in their lives—issues such as divorce, potty training, the death of a grandparent, or a move to a new town. Her findings led her to develop a model for "enhanced reference service," a librarian's approach to what mental health professionals might call bibliotherapy (Lu 2008).

An interesting study from the United Kingdom looked at the reasons why children's information needs might go unanswered, why information seeking might end in failure rather than success. Focusing particularly on cases where the child sought information from a person, Andrew Shenton (2007) found that five different factors contributed to information-seeking failure. The first of these factors was a need-source mismatch. The source from which the child sought information turned out to be inappropriate. Shenton gives the example of a six-year-old boy who asked his father, his mother, and his sister about the rules of soccer; none could answer his questions. Sometimes a reference source was too general or too specific to yield a satisfactory response.

Knowledge deficiency was the second factor in information-seeking failure. In these cases, the child didn't know enough about a subject to identify a suitable search term. Skills shortcomings were the third factor. Children lacked the skills needed to retrieve the information from a source at hand: they had difficulty using the index or dealing with an alphabetical list.

Psychological barriers were the fourth cause of information-seeking failure. Sometimes the child had trouble getting started on an information search because he wasn't even sure that the information existed. Other children were just overwhelmed by the demands of the information search. Shenton described children just flicking through the pages of a book without consulting an index or a table of contents; they couldn't motivate themselves to use a more fruitful strategy.

Finally, a related factor was social unease and inhibition. This emotional barrier arose most often when a child had to confront an adult to get the needed information. Usually prior experiences had convinced these children that they could not trust the adult or that the encounter would be uncomfortable.

Librarians who are aware of these obstacles that children face when seeking to satisfy information needs can respond in a variety of ways. They can make an effort to incorporate more effective information literacy instruction into everyday reference situations. They can be more sensitive to children who just assume that the library doesn't have any information because they were unsuccessful in identifying any useful source.

They can be more aware of children's limited frames of reference and knowledge bases. They can be sensitive to the questions that children are afraid or unable to articulate for themselves. And above all, they can be more approachable themselves. Good practice would dictate getting out from behind the public service desk and approaching children standing puzzled in front of bookshelves or leafing fruitlessly through books on the table.

Children's librarians should also be aware of the work done at the University of Washington on the everyday life information needs of tweens, children between the ages of 9 and 13 (Fisher et al. 2007). The researchers gathered in-depth qualitative data from two relatively small groups of tweens. They found that these youngsters are highly aware of their own everyday information needs as well as the value represented in a variety of information sources. The tweens believed that information seeking was a healthy and necessary activity but often a frustrating one because sources were difficult to access and communicate with and often failed to provide the best information to meet their needs. The challenge for librarians is clearly to find a way to be a trusted and reliable source of information for these children.

By far the most research related to children's information-seeking behavior has been in the context of computers and digital information resources. Some of this research, such as that conducted at UCLA in the early 1990s on the Science Library Catalog (Borgman et al. 1995; Walter and Borgman 1991), informed real-life library applications such as the commercial Kids Catalog. We learned from our controlled experiments and observations of children using the prototype Science Library Catalog that children search most effectively when they are able to work in an open-ended browsing mode. Their less developed keyboarding and spelling skills make even keyword searches problematical, and their limited frames of reference and knowledge base make subject searching difficult.

We have now learned quite a bit about how children go about looking for information in a digital environment. In her introduction to a special issue of *Library Trends* devoted to children's access and use of digital resources, Allison Druin (2005) points out that children today expect to find computers in libraries. However, software designers and information architects have not paid a lot of attention to creating interfaces and content that are developmentally appropriate — except, of course, on the popular commercial game sites designed to attract children to products as much as to an interactive digital environment. Many librarians observe — and sometimes complain — that children are not using library computers for information retrieval but rather for game sites. Others complain that kids do use computers for quick and easy information fixes when they have homework assignments, relying on a Google search or a Wikipedia article when a more extensive and sophisticated search would be a better choice.

Some researchers have suggested that one solution to the first problem—the greater allure of game sites than information sites—lies in involving children in the design process. Andrew Large and Jamshid Beheshti (2005), for example, have teased out a set of design guidelines for web portals based on their research with children. They recommend limiting the subject focus of a portal; using mental models or metaphors that children can relate to; developing a clear layout, bright colors, and an age-appropriate mascot; finding a name for the portal that resonates with kids; allowing for different retrieval options; and allowing for a great deal of interactivity and personalization.

Ultimately, the problem of children not using digital information resources effectively can really only be addressed through educational strategies. We know the set of skills needed to be an effective searcher and user of information, and we have some idea about the best ways to teach these information skills to children. The conventional wisdom is that people—adults as well as children—will be most likely to internalize these skills if they are taught in the context of a real-life information need. Thus, librarians look for both elementary and college students who have specific homework needs that require information to fulfill. These are the students most likely to absorb the lessons about search strategies, about methods of evaluating electronic information resources, and about integrating the information into one's own work without plagiarizing. We ordinarily assume that teaching these lessons is the job of the school librarian. Should children's librarians working in public libraries take any responsibility for teaching information literacy?

I have argued in the past that they should (Walter 1997, 2001, 2008). We can teach these skills informally while conducting reference interviews, in the same way that we used to "think aloud" while using a card catalog with children: "Let's see, let's try looking under Father Serra. Nope. That doesn't work. What about using his first name, too—is it Junipero Serra? Okay. This looks good." That kind of thing. The reference librarians at the new Main Library in Santa Monica have their computers on rotating platforms so they can swivel them around and show the patron at the desk what they are looking at. At the very least, learning by osmosis in a natural search environment like this can reinforce skills and search strategies learned elsewhere. Tutors in homework centers can also model good search and evaluation strategies as they work with students on actual assignments.

An IMLS-funded research project located at the St. Louis Public Library, Project CATE, involved children and teens in determining what young users needed to know in order to use digital resources appropriately. The investigators then developed an outcome-based approach to designing services that responded to their findings. These included a variety of educational offerings (Dresang 2005; Dresang, Gross, and Holt 2006). Other libraries should consider offering formal training opportunities for children and perhaps for their parents as well. These could be one-shot workshops on topics with currency and relevance: using the World Wide Web to research Martin Luther King Jr. or the Superbowl or baseball cards or some current pop star. What about running a summer computer camp? Or partnering with a local after-school program to offer a series of kid-friendly lessons to lead youngsters beyond Google?

The digital divide—the gap in computer access between the haves and the have-nots—has not yet been bridged. There may come a day when computers with high-speed broadband Internet connections are as common in households as televisions, but we're not there yet. In a recent issue brief, the Children's Partnership (2007) reported that compared to their peers in households with annual incomes over $75,000, children in households with annual incomes less than $15,000 are one-half as likely to have a computer at home, one-third as likely to have the Internet at home, and one-seventh as likely to have broadband at home. Our commitment to equal access to all children is yet another reason that librarians must have a proactive approach to providing their young patrons with total connectivity and the skills to use it wisely.

Twenty-first-century children's librarians have information on their radar screens. They have seen their library schools become information schools and their reference desks receive new signage that reads "information," often in jazzy neon lights. They see firsthand evidence of the national statistics that children ask more questions than adults do (PLA 1997). We might worry that children don't always get the respect they deserve in their encounters with adult reference librarians, but we do our best to integrate this information role into our menu of services.

Over the past one hundred years, we have also institutionalized partnerships and collaborations as a best practice. We will discuss this aspect of library service to children next.

Leveraging Partnerships and Collaborations

Librarians have shown themselves to be consummate networkers over the years. Within the profession, we have established multitype library networks and consortia as well as the kinds of complex agreements that made it possible to adopt the MARC record as the basis for online catalogs worldwide. The 1960s focus on outreach described in chapter 1 led to a renewed effort to form partnerships with other community organizations—nonprofit, government, and commercial. More recently, funding agencies such as IMLS have mandated that libraries preparing grant proposals include significant partnership components. Because of its joint mission to develop both museum and library services, IMLS placed a particularly high value on partnerships between these two organizations. The results have sometimes been a little forced, but more often these collaborations produced useful synergies.

In January 2005, the Urban Libraries Council surveyed the children's and youth services librarians in its member libraries for a census of best practices in a number of areas, including partnerships. The results revealed a broad range of community partners: schools; symphony orchestras; the United Way; sports teams; museums; Boys and Girls Clubs; other government agencies, including jails, parks and recreation programs, health departments, and housing authorities; museums; foundations; and businesses (Walter et al. 2005). It was not possible to determine, however, the degree to which these collaborations reflect deep, strategic alliances. Some of the organizations listed as partners appeared to be financial sponsors or targets of outreach efforts, rather than true collaborative partners.

Whatever the level of involvement, effective partnerships require an investment in time and resources. The most effective and lasting collaborations involve both an initial and ongoing commitment to maintaining communication channels that build respect and trust among the partners. Ongoing partnerships also tend to develop deep levels of interaction and integration between the various players. In a classic *Harvard Business Review* article, Rosabeth Moss Kanter (1994) identified five levels of integration that characterize productive partner relationships:

1. Strategic integration, involving continuing contact among the top leaders and policy makers. Sometimes new governance structures emerge to facilitate this integration.
2. Tactical integration, bringing professionals together to develop plans for specific projects.

3. Operational integration, providing ways to get the work done on a daily basis.

4. Interpersonal integration, building the foundations for creating future synergies and values.

5. Cultural integration, involving the communication skills, cultural awareness, and deep commitment to bridge differences and create a new culture.

My observation of children's library collaborations across the country is that most of them operate at either the strategic or operational levels of integration. It is fairly standard practice for youth services coordinators or managers to meet with their counterparts in the local school system, for example. These tend to be networking events in which participants exchange information about the activities of each organization. Frontline staff then work out the details of actual joint programs such as class visits or shared websites or summer reading lists. Many short-term grant-funded projects never go past the tactical and operational levels, with professionals from both organizations coming together to make an event happen or a product be produced. Kanter (1994) identified three essential aspects of more lasting partnerships:

1. They must yield real benefits for both partners.

2. They must create new value rather than mere exchange in which each partner gets something back for what it puts in.

3. They develop dense webs of interpersonal connections and internal infrastructures that enhance learning.

The Philadelphia Partnership for Peace, a project funded by IMLS, is an interesting example of a project-oriented partnership between the Free Library of Philadelphia, the Atwater Kent Museum (devoted to the history of the city of Philadelphia), WXPN-FM (a public radio station), and the House of Umoja (a grass-roots, community-based organization). These very different nonprofit institutions formed a partnership to help combat the youth violence that plagues their city. Each partner was responsible for accomplishing a unique objective. The House of Umoja was committed to creating an educational DVD highlighting its own history of antiviolence initiatives and to reaching an ambitious quantitative goal of new young people who had signed the Imani pledge to abstain from violence. The Atwater Kent Museum agreed to curate an exhibition about the history of nonviolence efforts in Philadelphia and then to create small kiosks based on that exhibition for five Free Library branches. WXPN-FM produced a radio series that featured local storytellers sharing tales woven from facts about the House of Umoja, the ancient African city of Djenne, and principles of nonviolence. The Free Library created a curriculum related to nonviolence and alternative strategies for conflict resolution that could be used in its LEAP after-school programs. In addition, the library was responsible for administering the grant as a whole.

In addition to the four goals just listed, the IMLS proposal included a fifth component, the creation of an ongoing partnership between the four participating organizations that would continue to work collectively to address complex issues such as youth violence.

Interestingly, the very structure of the project, with each agency responsible for its own separate program, precluded the kinds of integration that Kanter suggested are required for ongoing collaboration. There was little need to work together once the partners had all agreed on the parameters of the project. With the exception of the original unrealistic objective of 100,000 signed Imani pledges that proved impossible to reach, each agency accomplished its goal. However, the principals from each agency had mixed assessments of the viability of the coalition as an ongoing collaboration. It had proved difficult to coordinate the efforts of four organizations with such different capacities and cultures, and there was little incentive to do so because each agency had its own separate project element on which to focus. The library had interpreted its role as grant administrator very literally, monitoring the progress of each project element and managing the budget. In retrospect, the principals from the four organizations agreed that they should have spent more time building confidence and trust among themselves and developing ongoing informal as well as formal communication channels.

There are at least two reasons to believe that collaboration will continue to be a significant element in the way that children's librarians do their work. The first is the funding climate, which will almost certainly continue to mandate partnerships. The second is that children's librarians are still passionate advocates and missionaries who believe so strongly in the importance of their work that they will usually leap at any opportunity to develop alliances that will spread the good word. They just need to be reminded to look for collaborations that are truly strategic.

In addition to the six original principles of library service to children that were reconsidered in chapter 2 and the two more recent principles discussed here, there are two other principles or trends that should be considered. Neither of these has had the salience or the enduring qualities of the others, but I believe that they have a particular relevance to our moment in history and to twenty-first-century children. These principles are

- Library use is a civic activity.
- Americans and American libraries have a responsibility to look beyond their borders and to adopt a global perspective

Library Use Is a Civic Activity

The civic role of the American public library is surprisingly elusive for a publicly funded institution that has often rationalized its existence on its support for our country's democratic values and practices. One of the clearest expressions of the library's potential for providing civic benefits is found in the document that laid out the objectives for the Boston Public Library in 1852. The trustees acknowledged that the library would supply books for people who could not afford to buy them. This was important, they claimed, because it would raise the conditions of those reading individuals and would strengthen the very foundations of our democratic society. Here are their words:

> For it has been rightly judged that, — under political, social and religious institutions like ours, — it is of paramount importance that the means of general information should be so diffused that the largest possible number of persons should be induced to read and understand questions going down to the very foundations of social order, which are constantly presenting themselves, and which we, as a people are constantly required to decide, and do decide, either ignorantly, or wisely. (*Upon the objects* 1852, 15)

From its very beginning, therefore, the public library was associated with the development of the informed citizenry that is necessary to the functioning of an effective democracy. Later, library professionals would extend this to a passionate advocacy of the First Amendment right to intellectual freedom and its opposition to censorship.

Almost all of the civic activities in which public libraries have engaged over the years have been aimed at adults: candidate forums and distribution of election materials and voter registration forms, usually grudging distribution of tax forms, citizenship classes for new immigrants. Very little has been documented about libraries' role in developing children's civic values or civic literacy or encouraging them to think about their role as citizens.

A rare exception is a program that Annette Simpson created for the second through fifth graders who participate in her after-school Great Adventurers series at the Monrovia Public Library in California. She runs three seven-week Great Adventurers series each year. In fall 2008, during the height of election fever here in the United States, the Great Adventurers participated in a program to "Vote for Books." Using inexpensive promotional materials from Upstart, simple prizes, and homemade props, the children came together once a week to have fun while they learned more about the American electoral process. Each week the librarian read a book about a president, and the children formed teams to play games that generated knowledge and interest in topics such as the electoral college and presidential trivia. The overarching activity, however, was a simulated presidential campaign, with books as stand-ins for candidates. By the fifth session, the primaries were over, and the candidates had been narrowed down to the top two: *Charlotte's Web* and the Magic Tree House Series. A child who was passionate about each was chosen to be its campaign manager. Children lobbied for their favorites, and at the sixth session, they voted. At the seventh and final meeting, the librarian ceremoniously counted the votes, and the Magic Tree House was declared the winner.

We could do a lot in our public libraries to help children practice democratic skills and to empower them to be active members of their communities. I will discuss this at some length in chapter 4. Chapter 4 will also include a rationale—almost a manifesto—for thinking globally. Let me just introduce the topic here.

Americans and American Libraries Have a Responsibility to Look beyond Their Borders and to Adopt a Global Perspective

As locally funded government organizations, public libraries have always emphasized local services that meet local needs. International concerns rarely resonate much at the neighborhood level. When they do, it is usually because there are local connections to international events. Thus, immigration patterns link American communities—and their public libraries—to countries of origin. Americans rarely pay much attention to wars on foreign soil unless we have soldiers fighting there or we become responsible for refugees from those wars. Recent events, starting with the attack on the World Trade Center in New York on September 11, 2001, may have begun to change the somewhat isolated and parochial world-views held by many of us. I will argue in the next chapter that we have an obligation to help our children take their place as global citizens in a world of permeable borders and shrinking distances. For now, I will just review some examples of specific library efforts to adopt a more international approach to services for children.

Librarians in urban areas with large immigrant populations apparently made conscious efforts to make newcomer children feel at home. Frances Clarke Sayers writes:

> Long before the neighboring glass house of the United Nations ennobled the East River of New York, the Central Children's Room dramatized its allegiance to internationalism not only in its book collection, its staff, and its exhibitions, but also in its daily responses to the children and adults of the multi-nationed city. (1972, 148–49)

She goes on to describe a major international exhibition mounted in 1933 at NYPL in association with the Metropolitan Museum of Art. The scope appears to have been entirely European; there is no record that other parts of the world were represented.

The 1930s, when the whole world seemed united in economic woes if nothing else, were a time when children's book publishers and librarians shared an interest in promoting international understanding. Four of the ten Newbery winners named in the 1930s are set in other countries: *The Cat Who Went to Heaven* by Elizabeth Coatsworth (Japan), *Young Fu of the Upper Yangtze* by Elizabeth Lewis (China), *Dobry* by Monica Shannon (Bulgaria), and *The White Stag* by Kate Seredy (Hungary). Only eleven books published since 1940 and set in other countries have received the Newbery Medal (ALSC n.d.-d). This fairly ethnocentric worldview has been alleviated to some degree by the establishment of the Mildred Batchelder Award in 1966, given by ALSC to "an American publisher for a children's book considered to be the most outstanding translated book of the year" (Kruse 2008).

The award honors Mildred L. Batchelder, a former executive secretary of ALA's Children's Services Division who was convinced of the need for children to be exposed to books from many parts of the world. She believed that knowing the children's stories of a country leads to an understanding of its people and helps readers feel close to the children who are reading the stories in other lands (Batchelder 1972). Since 1968, when the first award winner was announced, books from Germany, Norway, Greece, Holland, Russia, Denmark, Sweden, Japan, Israel, Italy, Spain, and France have been honored (ALSC n.d.-a).

There are at least three examples of Americans playing significant roles in facilitating library services for children in other countries. The first of these was the establishment of children's libraries in Brussels and Paris after World War I. These libraries were the brainchild of a group of American women who wanted to recognize the courage of Belgian and French children during the Great War and to help in educational reconstruction in the aftermath of that war. The most well known of these, L'Heure Joyeuse, was established in Paris in 1924. Based on American models in its design and services, it featured open stacks—an innovation in France at that time—and a welcoming environment for children. It was the first French municipal library to open its doors to children and stimulated what Mary Niles Maack (1993) has called a paradigm shift in French public library service. Elsewhere in France at that time, Anne Carroll Moore and an NYPL colleague, Jessie Carson, set up five model libraries in Aisne, each with a small children's section. Carson also trained the young French women recruited to work in those libraries, schooling them in the principles of children's librarianship that she and Moore had pioneered in the United States.

We cannot claim Jella Lepman, the remarkable woman instrumental in the founding of both the International Board on Books for Young People (IBBY) and the International Youth Library in Munich. Lepman was actually born in Germany and ended her life as a British subject living in Switzerland. However, during World War II, she served in the American Army and worked to develop cultural and educational programs for women and children in the American Zone in Germany after the war. Her vision for war-ravaged children was a world of the imagination fed by nourishing books. She was evidently a persuasive fund-raiser and enlisted the aid of many powerful organizations and political figures, including Eleanor Roosevelt, in the founding first of the International Youth Library in 1949 and then of IBBY in 1951 (International Youth Library n.d.; Lepman 1969). The International Youth Library exists to this day and features a collection of books from all over the world and a variety of cultural and educational programs.

A final example of American involvement in libraries for children overseas is the Lubuto Project. Jane Kinney Meyers, an American librarian whose husband's work took her to Lusaka, Zambia, saw the need for educational opportunities of all kinds for the homeless children living on their own in the streets of her city. Working with a nongovernmental organization that provided social services to these children, she established a library at the Fountain of Hope drop-in shelter. A twenty-foot, used shipping container was adapted to be the library, which soon contained thousands of books donated by individuals, schools, and publishers in the United States and the United Kingdom. Since that first makeshift library, the Lubuto Library Project has opened its first real library in a permanent structure and aspires to establish more throughout the region (www.lubuto.org/about.html). Denise Agosto (2008) writes that the Lubuto library functions as an information gateway for young people who are unable to go to school and as a space for positive social interactions.

These are inspiring stories of American philanthropy and initiative being put to work on behalf of children and libraries in other parts of the world. Although these are unidirectional initiatives, we Americans could also learn from what is being done well in other countries if we paid more attention to what is going on beyond our borders. Scandinavian countries are innovating with information technology in their children's libraries. Libraries in Croatia offer quality early childhood experiences in well-equipped playrooms in all of their public libraries. Librarians in many African countries not only circulate the books about HIV/AIDS and other desperately needed topics to their young people, they also write and publish those books.

There are a few institutional channels that American librarians can use to get more involved in global issues. ALSC has an International Relations Committee responsible for maintaining relationships with international organizations and fostering global awareness within the profession. Along with YALSA, ALSC has a representative on the United States Board on Books for Young People (USBBY), the United States national section of the International Board on Books for Young People (IBBY). IBBY was founded to promote international understanding through books for children and teenagers (http://usbby.org). The ALA representatives on the board host a program at the ALA Annual Conference that showcases a noted author whose books have a significant international dimension.

ALSC also nominates a representative to the Standing Committees of the Libraries for Children and Young Adults Section and the Literacy and Reading Section of the International Federation of Library Associations and Institutions (IFLA). Unfortunately, few American children's librarians are able to attend the expensive IFLA conferences, held throughout the world in August, when airfares are at their highest. These international connections help to link American library associations with international organizations whose goals and missions also focus on children and reading. It is not clear, however, that the consequences of these relationships trickle down to frontline librarians.

I will argue in the next chapter that today's children are citizens of the world, not just our own country, and that they deserve to have library services that reflect the interconnectedness of the world in which they live.

FOUR

The Children We Serve

IN *CHILDREN AND LIBRARIES: GETTING IT RIGHT* (WALTER 2001), I PRO-posed three alternative visions or concepts for the children we would be serving as we moved into the twenty-first century. These included the original notion of the child reader, an idea that inspired and guided the founders of library service to children. I suggested that we should also consider the child of the information age and the child in the community as we looked at our evolving place as librarians working a hundred years later. In this chapter, we will revisit those three concepts of the child and look at two additional notions of childhood that might usefully inform our thinking today. These new ideas are "the global child" and "the empowered child." Each of these five concepts of the child leads to a different approach to library service. All are plausible; all are hopeful; all are obtainable. They may not be mutually exclusive, but I have found it helpful to think about them separately. Each is based on a different understanding of the child who will shape and claim the future of the twenty-first century.

The Child as Reader

The library for the child reader is the vision that offers the most continuity with the past. It builds on the core values and visions of the librarians who founded library services for children in this country. It is consistent with the niche that these services have traditionally occupied. It is therefore a conservative vision, in the sense that it conserves a cherished and valued tradition.

As we think about the future of library service to children, however, we must look at even our most cherished and valued traditions to see how they hold up against today's realities. Can we be sure that books and reading will continue to be valued by our society? Will parents, educators, and policy makers continue to believe that books and reading are essential to the healthy development of children? Will voters agree that providing books and promoting reading for children are appropriate and necessary functions for tax-supported public libraries? I am writing these words during the worst economic recession our country has known for decades, when even the most basic government services are threatened. Will we librarians be able to make a case for the importance of books and reading in the lives of children?

I often challenge the students in my children's literature classes to come up with a personal top ten list of reasons for children to read fine literature today. It is an exercise I often put to myself as well. Here are some of the responses:

1. Reading builds vocabulary; it gives children words to think with.
2. Reading extends a child's experiences beyond his or her own household, block, and community.
3. Reading together creates a bond between the parent or caregiver and a very young child.
4. The child who reads becomes a member of the community of readers.
5. Stories give children and adults shared frames of reference.
6. Reading exercises the brain.
7. Children need stories to help them understand the narrative of their own lives.
8. Printed stories allow children to participate at their own pace, to pause and reflect or even skip over parts. Movies, our other great narrative form, move along at a more relentless pace.
9. Reading brings pleasure and delight.
10. Reading is empowering: it allows children to choose the narratives on which they want to spend time.

Lynne Sharon Schwartz (1997) writes eloquently about that tenth reason:

> So much of a child's life is lived for others. We [as children] learn what [adults] want us to learn, and show our learning for their gratification. All the reading I did as a child, behind closed doors, sitting on the bed while the darkness fell around me, was

an act of reclamation. This and only this I did for myself. This
was the way to make my life my own. (119)

It has been interesting to observe the profession's effort to build a
rational foundation for our reading mission. I wrote about the library faith
in chapter 1, a deeply held but unproven belief in the power of reading
"good" books as a means of improving human nature and presumably
human behavior as well. The world we operate in now seems to require
something more than blind faith, and children's librarians have dutifully
looked for research findings that bolster their claims of doing good work
and providing meaningful service.

One of the more significant initiatives, covered in some detail in
chapter 2, has been "Every Child Ready to Read," the ALSC/PLA joint
initiative to educate parents and caregivers in techniques they can use to
transfer critical emergent literacy skills to their preschool children. The
association leaders responsible for the original program drew on research
findings from the National Reading Panel and even hired academics with
impeccable credentials to design the workshop curricula. Not satisfied
with that, they commissioned a research study to determine whether the
research-based curriculum achieved its desired learning and behavior
outcomes (ALSC & PLA 2003). That study showed that parents of every
age, educational background, income level, and ethnicity who attended
the ECRR workshops significantly increased those behaviors that research
has shown stimulate reading readiness in young children. So we're feeling like we're on pretty solid ground here, at least in our efforts to improve
literacy in young children. The big lesson we learned is that we can't do
this job alone; we need to enlist caregivers and especially parents as the
child's first and best teachers.

At first I was a little unnerved when I read in *Freakonomics* (Levitt and Dubner 2005, 158–60) that rigorous statistical manipulation of
the data in the Early Childhood Longitudinal Study, conducted by the
U.S. Department of Education in the late 1990s, showed no correlation
between a child's being read to regularly and his or her early childhood
reading test scores. After all, the value of reading to children early and
often is another of our cherished beliefs. "Read to your bunny twenty
minutes a day," we proclaim. In 1985, a national Commission on Reading examined more than ten thousand research reports and concluded:
"The single most important activity for building the knowledge required
for eventual success in reading is reading aloud to children" (Anderson
et al. 1985, 23). The pediatricians who started Reach Out and Read, a

national nonprofit organization that promotes reading aloud by making books a routine part of pediatric care, seem to believe this. Their website reads: "Reach Out and Read trains doctors and nurses to advise parents about the importance of reading aloud and to give books to children at pediatric checkups from 6 months to 5 years of age" (www.reachoutand read.org/about.html). Maybe Levitt and Dubner were just missing some important data points.

According to Levitt and Dubner, the factor that *does* correlate with positive test scores is the presence of many books in the home. This shouldn't surprise us either. Stephen D. Krashen (2004) has been telling us this for years. However, he goes even farther and cites research that demonstrates that the more access kids have to books—in the classroom, in the school library, in the public library, and at home—the more likely they are to read. This makes such stunning common sense that you almost wonder why anybody bothered to test this notion, but they have, and it is true. Furthermore—and this is really good news for libraries— children get most of their books from libraries (Krashen 2004, 64ff). So we have some research evidence that backs up the importance of providing children with easy access to books from public and school libraries. Easy access to books does appear to correlate with the reading habit.

We seem to be on fairly firm ground in demonstrating our role—not central, perhaps, but not insignificant either—in leading children to books and reading. There is still a piece missing, however. Although librarians and some parents may value reading and the library's role in promoting childhood reading, the question remains: is reading still considered an essential skill and a desirable lifetime habit? The alarming results of the 2004 National Endowment for the Arts (NEA) study on the reading habits of Americans would suggest not (Literary reading in dramatic decline 2004). That study showed an overall decline of ten percentage points in literary readers from 1982 to 2002, and the decline in literary reading by the youngest adults, those ages 18 to 24, was 55 percent greater than that of the total adult population. An update to the 2004 study released in January 2009 was more optimistic. This new study showed that for the first time in twenty-five years, American adults were reading more literature than they had before, and young adults showed the most dramatic increases in their literary reading (More American adults read literature 2009). Still, only a slight majority of American adults read literature or books in any format, according to the report.

The NEA findings lead me to think that we should pay more attention to the value added to young lives through reading, to learning how much reliance we can put on our list of the top ten reasons for children to read. Are we just twenty-first-century believers in the same old "library faith" that sustained Anne Carroll Moore and Mary Wright Plummer? It is the children's librarians who seem to be the most avid devotees of the faith today. Many public library administrators have responded to the apparent decline in reading by restocking shelves with DVDs instead of books, by removing shelves to make room for computers with Internet access, and by redefining young adult services as a portal to manga, anime, and computer games.

So much of what we children's librarians do in our everyday work is an affirmation of our belief that reading is not a lost art or a dying skill but rather an essential element of being human in an advanced civilization, that being human today in the United States also means being literate.

I have found personal inspiration and validation in *Proust and the Squid: The Story and Science of the Reading Brain* by Maryanne Wolf (2007). The author is a professor of child psychology at Tufts University, and her book is a celebration of reading as one of the most remarkable inventions in history and as one of the most remarkable achievements of any individual who masters it. There is much to learn from Wolf's examination of reading and its effects on the history of civilization. She also looks at how the act of reading actually affects the structure of the brain. She makes the point that although the brain is hardwired for the acquisition of language, reading must be learned anew by every human child. And learning to decode the alphabet changes the brain in dramatic ways. When a person learns how to read, that person's brain is forever changed, both physiologically and intellectually. Underlying the brain's ability to learn to read is its astonishing capacity to make connections among structures and circuits originally devoted to other, more basic brain processes such as vision and language.

The physiological significance of reading is enormous. However, Wolf is equally adamant about the significance of the personal and intellectual dimensions of reading, of the content of what we read. She reminds us that much of what we think and how we think is based on what we read. She quotes author Joseph Epstein: "'A biography of any literary person ought to deal at length with what he read and when, for in some sense, *we are what we read*'" (Wolf 2007, 5). In that case, I am the product of Tasha Tudor's *Mother Goose*, Johanna Spyri's *Heidi*, Carl Sandberg's *Rootabaga Stories*, the Nancy Drew mysteries, Louisa May Alcott's *Little Women*, *The Diary of Anne Frank*, Jane Austen's *Pride and Prejudice*, Robert Pirsig's *Zen and the Art of Motorcycle Maintenance*, Thomas Mann's *The*

Magic Mountain, *Mastering the Art of French Cooking* by Julia Child, Louisette Bertholle, and Simone Beck, Toni Morrison's *The Bluest Eye*, Susan Patron's *The Higher Power of Lucky*, hundreds of adult mystery novels, and every citation in the reference list for this book.

If we are going to design our services primarily for the reading child, we will need to be as passionate about the value of reading as our fore-mothers were. We will need to remind ourselves and the policy makers who control our funding that reading is an essential skill as we move farther into the twenty-first century and reading good books builds our capacity to think and feel in ways that are central to defining who we are as humans. This may be especially true in childhood. In the book about her own reading and rereading of the Narnia books throughout her life, Laura Miller (2008) quotes the novelist Graham Greene: "'Perhaps it is only in childhood that books have any deep influence on our lives. In later life we admire, we are entertained, we may modify some views we already hold, but we are more likely to find in books merely a confirmation of what is in our minds already. . . . But in childhood all books are books of divination, telling us about the future'" (7).

Sometimes it appears that twenty-first-century children are more likely to see their future in the computer games that fascinate them so. Whether they read what Eliza Dresang (1999) called "hand-held books" or not, computers are increasingly a big part of their lives. In the library, we have to consider services for these children of the information age.

The Child of the Information Age

As I noted in chapter 3, computers with their access to myriad digital resources have already changed the way we deliver many of our services to children. Children of the information age—boys in particular—have breached the walls and claimed their right to computers and the Internet. Never mind that they do not have all the rights that adult library patrons do; many, perhaps most, libraries use filtering software to screen content on computers in the children's room. Most young patrons probably don't care as much as we intellectual freedom advocates do; they are not there to access forbidden websites. They may not even want to access information sites at all. Mostly, librarians tell me and my own observations confirm, they want to play games.

We children's librarians tend to be a little dismissive of those computer and video games, unlike our colleagues in young adult services.

Sometimes it seems that the best rationale we can offer for this activity is that we encourage reading for pleasure. Why not computing for pleasure? We should probably pay more attention to voices like that of Steven Johnson (2005), who claims that computer games place heavy cognitive demands on their players. In fact, much of these games' captivation is due to the challenges they place on individuals to persist in their efforts to solve complex challenges. John C. Beck and Mitchell Wade (2004) go even farther. They insist that the hours spent playing video games have given young people now entering the workforce some unique and badly needed skills: an ability to multitask and a willingness to take risks. Those ten-year-old boys clustered around a computer in your children's room arguing about the best strategy for knocking out an opponent's avatar may be engaged in the same kind of reasoning twenty years from now in some corporate boardroom.

The Children's Partnership, a nonprofit organization that advocates for children's access to technology and health care, released an issue brief in March 2007 that made the case for children's greater access to broadband Internet connectivity. Their argument was based on four areas in which broadband, with its capacity to transfer large amounts of data and graphic content quickly, could improve children's lives: academic achievement, preparation for the workforce, health care, and civic participation. Most of the health-related applications are more relevant to teens than to younger children, but all school-age children can benefit from access to the most up-to-date digital opportunities.

The Children's Partnership urges policy makers to find ways to achieve universal broadband access. That goal may be even farther off now than it looked when the organization wrote its report in 2007. At least one city that the report cited for its effort to implement universal wireless connections—Philadelphia—has had to abandon the project because of unexpected technical problems and resource issues. After-school programs and public libraries are the logical places to bridge the digital divide until every family has full access.

However, access is only part of the problem. The other two issues that we need to think hard about are content and education for information literacy. And if we are going to fully realize the potential of this marvelous device that Seymour Papert (1993) called "the children's machine," we also need to consider how we are going to integrate computers and digital resources into our services and collections.

There is now plenty of appropriate content on the World Wide Web for children who are looking for information to satisfy personal interests or homework needs. Much of this content is highlighted on Great Web Sites for Kids, a project of one hard-working ALSC committee (ALSC n.d.-c). The librarians on this committee have even found ten worthwhile sites in Spanish. The problem is not that the content doesn't exist; the problem is motivating children to use the Great Web Sites instead of automatically going to Wikipedia or the first site that pops up on Google.

Almost every public library has a website that serves as a portal to librarian-approved and selected websites such as the ALSC list. I have never seen any research that would document children's use of the book-marked sites that librarians provide for them. Even the best of these are a little indirect or cumbersome. A child looking for information on a specific national park, for example, needs to delve down deep into the architecture of the bookmarks before finding something useful on Yellowstone or Yosemite. And if she's looking for information on a relatively obscure animal or person, she may not find the information there at all. Logging on to Google or entering the search term into Wikipedia is so much easier, even if the information is possibly less reliable. Google may even correct the child's spelling.

Of course, even the rapidly proliferating kid-friendly and kid-appropriate informational content on the World Wide Web is rarely as good as what the library probably has on its shelves in print sources of all kinds unless the topic is a current event. For young people who read below sixth-grade level, books written for children are more likely to be understood than digital content.

In addition to the gazillions of websites available on the World Wide Web, most libraries subscribe to digital databases that may have information that is useful to children. Here the problem of access is compounded. Children must know about the database and they must know how to use its particular search protocol.

Good children's librarians are accustomed to guiding children to sources on the shelves of their libraries. Most will spot a child who looks puzzled or lost while wandering through the stacks. They are less likely to intervene when a child is at the computer. We may need to rethink our assumptions about children's capacity and competence. Yes, they are digital natives; computers and the Internet have been around since before they were born. This doesn't mean they know how to use them effectively any more than a teenager can drive a car at sixteen without instruction and practice.

Back in the early days of the Internet, when people still called it the information superhighway, the Enoch Pratt Public Library in Baltimore offered an eight-week course that gave children both the confidence and the competence to use e-mail, chat, library catalogs, and the World Wide Web. Trained volunteers provided the instruction, and when the kids had finished their training, they were "licensed to drive" (Mondowney 1997).

Few public libraries offer that kind of intense information literacy instruction to children. We tend to assume that schools are providing these tools. However, we do children a disservice when we mistake their ease with the computer for effectiveness. They do need our help in deciding when they need good information instead of the handiest. They need our help finding the best resources for their needs, whether it's in print or on the Web. They need our help figuring out what sound and useful information looks like on a web page. They need our help integrating that digital information with what they already know about the subject and presenting it in their report or work sheet without plagiarizing. They need our help in learning how to properly cite those web and other digital resources.

In chapter 3, I highlighted a number of ways that we can provide that help. We can be more proactive about approaching children who are using the computers to search for information. We can be more transparent when helping a child locate digital information, offering useful pointers about evaluating a website. Our homework center staff can consciously work in mini-lessons in information literacy while they help children with reports. And yes, we can offer occasional workshops. Many parents would welcome this kind of educational offering at the library, and children would be surprised at the world we could open up to them.

The same committee that maintains Great Web Sites for Kids posts their selection criteria for interested web surfers: authorship or sponsorship, purpose, design and stability, and content. These criteria could provide a starting place for librarians who want to help children and interested adults do a better job of evaluating online content. Each general criterion has several specific qualifiers. For example, the "Purpose" criterion includes the following guidelines for assessment:

- A site's purpose should be clear and its content should reflect its purpose, be it to entertain, persuade, educate, or sell.
- Advertising should be limited and appropriate.
- Sites devoted strictly to sales will not be considered as Great Sites.
- A good site should enrich the user's experience and expand the imagination. Sites promoting social biases rather than

enlarging the views of the child should not be considered Great Sites.

The Fairview Branch of the Santa Monica Public Library serves a large population of tweens, many of whom come from families whose primary language is Spanish. After school, the library is jammed with students vying for space at one of the eight laptop computers in the Youth Technology Center. Library policy dictates that homework use gets priority, and there are college students available to help with schoolwork. In addition to the one-on-one homework help, the library has at times offered a wide range of workshops, all designed to expose middle school students to the basic concepts of information literacy in a friendly and mostly entertaining way. One workshop on database searching, for example, was presented as a "CIA Assignment." The students pretended they were spies doing research on a country. Librarians at the branch also offer classes for Spanish-speaking parents to enable them to feel comfortable with the technology that their children are using and to introduce them to resources that might be helpful in their own lives (Walter 2008).

Children of the information age may require new and different kinds of programming than the storytimes and puppet shows and author visits that have been our staples for child readers. These digital natives might want more hands-on activities involving computer graphics and animation. They may want to produce content for the Web as well as use it. They might respond to an initiative to link up via webcams with children at a library across the country—or across the ocean. We know that they love the interactivity of the most engaging websites; we need to build that interactivity into our own websites and programming. Some librarians around the country are doing this. The Children and Technology Committee has posted a list of great technology programs for children on the ALSC wiki, with links to learn more. Several of these programs—Animated Authors from Cuyahoga County Public Library in Ohio, Scratch for eight- to eleven-year-olds at Hennepin County Library in Minnesota, and StoryTubes at the Gail Borden Public Library in Illinois, for example— offer opportunities for children to create online content (ALSC n.d.-b).

As we become more adept at integrating information and communications technologies into our services, we will also become more effective at seamlessly weaving our print and digital collections into one coherent whole. Our colleagues in academic libraries are already skilled at balancing digital and print resources. Their catalogs, admittedly much more complex to navigate than anything we would want to offer to children, point patrons to both sources. They routinely offer classes and workshops to faculty and students who want to become more proficient consumers of digital resources. It is time for us to be more intentional about our acquisition and management of digital resources for children.

Digital resources have the potential to take children to virtual worlds far from home. Still, children live in their real communities, and we can learn a lot about serving them better if we keep this fact in mind.

The Child in the Community

Although the founders of library service to children designed their services to promote books and reading, they still understood the importance of their young patrons' environment. Librarians working in rural areas pondered schemes to bring books to children in remote farmhouses far from the nearest library. Urban librarians were concerned about crowded tenements and unsafe sweatshops where children labored for pennies. In a speech to the American Library Association in 1905, Frances Jenkins Olcott, then head of the children's department of the Carnegie Library of Pittsburgh, talked about the demographics of her city, where more than two-thirds of the total population of 321,616 were "either foreign born, or children of foreign born parents, and persons of negro descent" (72). Olcott was knowledgeable about the employment opportunities, the housing conditions, and the curriculum of the public schools. She knew the city inside and out, and she understood what living there was like for children.

Olcott knew that the Carnegie Library was reaching thousands of children through its branches and through the city schools. She worried about the large numbers of children who didn't come into the library and were not enrolled in school. "These children work at home," she explained, "in toby shops, in factories, or they sell papers. There are also 'gangs' of restless boys who hang about street corners and whose lawless mischief leads them into crime" (73). Olcott did not abandon these at-risk children. She organized an initiative that cooperated with "institutions for social betterment," such as social settlements, the juvenile court, and the Newsboys' Home. Library staff established home libraries—small cases of books—in working-class homes. During home visits, librarians would gather a group of children from the neighborhood and talk about the books, read aloud, tell stories, and organize crafts such as sewing or basketry. "The visitor from the library has a strong influence upon the home in which her group meets, as well as among the neighbors," Olcott explained. "She is often able to aid the families in case of illness, poverty, or lack of work, by putting them in touch with charitable institutions" (74).

Outreach—or social work? Librarians sometimes embrace the first activity and shun the second. Yet when they truly begin to plan and implement programs that take into account the communities in which children live, the lines tend to blur. Traditional library missions may expand when we go beyond superficial marketing studies or environmental scans and really dig for insights into our communities.

We will rarely find those useful insights if we stay sequestered behind the walls of our library buildings. I understand the competing demands of reference desk schedules, storytimes, and staff meetings. In spite of those very real constraints, time must be found for walking in the footsteps of the children and families whom we serve. Only then can we begin to truly understand the circumstances of their lives and respond with the very best and most relevant services, books, and information in all of its many formats.

The outreach services of the 1960s and 1970s brought children's librarians out into the communities in search of potential library patrons. I remember telling stories in the playground of the housing project near the branch library where I worked in San Francisco in the late 1960s. It was eye opening to see how many children living just three blocks away had never found their way to the local library until I found my way to them. A few years later I had moved to Southern California and worked for several years at the Malabar Branch Library in the Boyle Heights barrio. My colleagues and I tried everything we could think of to reach out to the Latino families in our neighborhood. We organized mother's clubs and community *posadas*. We worked with local women to make piñatas to sell at the *feria de los niños* in the park. We shopped at the local markets and ate lunch at Manuel's, home of the famous Hollenbeck burrito. One of my daughters went to summer camp with the local girls club, and my father helped the kids make a huge Frankenstein for the library's summer reading program. It was outreach based on person-to-person contacts as we tried to design library services that would be meaningful to the children and families in our community. It was also outreach that cost nothing but our time.

We librarians spent a lot of time outside the walls of the Malabar Branch as we forged those contacts. Like those early librarians in Pittsburgh, we were even welcomed into people's homes. We knew people's names, and they knew us. We also looked for new ways to invite the people into *our* home, the library. Sometimes it happened serendipitously.

I still remember one hot summer day at the library. The children had decided to hold a yard sale to raise money for a field trip. Families had pitched in to donate the usual unwanted household items and old clothes. There were used books and old tape cassettes. People drifted in and out. As the afternoon wore on, mothers came by to check on their children. Then the fathers came by to check on their wives. Somebody brought a portable boom box and started playing mariachi music. Soon it was a full-fledged *tardeada*, an afternoon party. Was this the dreaded phenomenon of "mission creep"? Or did the little library with its precious grassy backyard play a role in a precious moment of community building? Did the mothers and fathers who came to the library that day feel a little more ownership of this unfamiliar American institution that had already attracted their children? I think so, and I think this was a transcendent example of the library as a public space.

More recently, I was privileged to observe the family storytime at the Venice branch of the Los Angeles Public Library. I was acting as a participant observer in order to conduct research on this particular service. I attended every session in my roles as the mother of the librarian and a member of the community as well as a researcher. Over time, the families came to accept my presence. Eva is a lively, competent storyteller, and she had a large, faithful audience of moms and dads and children ranging from babes in arms to six- and seven-year-old siblings of the preschoolers who were the target audience. Children who arrived early knew to set out the mats at the front of the children's room. Moms and dads settled in the chairs in the back. After the storytime, everybody moved to the low tables for simple crafts. Parents helped the children paste and color and chatted with each other. This is a scene that could be observed at libraries around the country.

But pay attention to what is going on among the parents. Venice is home to a lot of people who work in the entertainment industry, and there was a lot of shop talk among parents who knew each other professionally or who welcomed the networking opportunity. There were several older white couples that had adopted Chinese daughters; they shared resources with each other, and they were very pleased when I brought my Taiwanese doctoral student along.

I was intrigued with the community that I saw develop as the year went on. In the spring, there was much talk about kindergarten. What about the local public schools? Was it too late to get into a good private school? In the summer, there were visitors—grandparents and cousins from out of town. Then it was fall. At the first storytimes after September 11, 2001, there was a lot of anxious talk about the children's responses to this event and what parents could or should do. One mother was worried because her little boy kept building towers of blocks and knocking them down, over and over again, even flying his toy planes into them. Another mother, an experienced preschool teacher, reassured her neighbor. This was important, she said. It was a way for him to process the event and reduce it to actions he could understand. This kind of informal information sharing led to a good discussion and seemed to reassure some of the parents.

We say that we provide family storytime because it is a way to share books and literacy experiences with young children and to model book-sharing techniques with parents. What I came to understand as I observed the family storytime at the Venice Library was that it also built community. It created a public space for busy parents to gather with other busy parents in an activity that was good for their children and made the adults feel that they were doing the right thing. On Monday evenings, the Venice Library was a significant hub in a fragile web of community supports for Venice families.

Every community will have its own character and its own ways of interacting with the library. Cookie-cutter approaches to library service will not work in our diverse communities in small towns, suburbs, farmlands, and cities across the country. In the next chapter, I will suggest some ways that children's librarians can dig for the knowledge they need to understand those communities and then to plan and implement services that get it right for the children who live there.

For now, let us look beyond a child's home, block, and neighborhood to consider yet another concept of childhood with much broader parameters, the global child.

The Global Child

It was nearly fifty years ago that Marshall McLuhan was writing about the emergence of the global village as electronic media transformed the world with instant communications between every part of the globe. I was reading his *Understanding Media* in the late 1960s at the same time that I was watching news broadcast directly from the battlefronts in Vietnam. American soldiers fighting in those faraway jungles seemed so close.

It made the war and the suffering it caused very real, and many of us were moved to protest our involvement there. Never again would the American military commanders allow reporters such free access to the front lines. Instead we were treated to views of surgical air strikes that looked like screens from a video game in the first Iraq War, the phenomenon of "embedded" reporters in the second. Television has indeed shrunk the world to a global village and helped us to feel that what happens in far-away countries has consequences here.

The world feels more interconnected all the time. The increasing urgency of global warming has alerted us to both the fragility and the importance of those connections. Our economic system is now international as well. Banks fail in New York, and stock markets in Japan, Hong Kong, and Europe shudder along with our own. And sadly, war continues to remind us that we are all citizens of one world. Children of military families become very familiar with places on the map that were unknown to most Americans before we sent soldiers there: Somalia, Afghanistan, and, of course, Iraq.

The United States continues to attract immigrants from all over the world, many coming for better economic opportunities, some for improved educational opportunities for their children. And we continue to offer a safe haven to refugees from many war-torn countries.

Minneapolis, where I spend a lot of time visiting my daughter's family, is home to a large Somali community. Across the river, St. Paul's Hmong community continues to grow. Ten years ago it was hard to find fresh tortillas in this northern Midwest city; now a surging Mexican American population has created a market for *tripa* and *barbacoa* as well as tortillas and salsa. Some of the lost boys of Darfur have also ended up in small towns in the Midwest, welcomed and supported initially by local churches. I sometimes wonder what they make of this cold climate and bleak winter landscape, so different from the desert country they left behind.

It is no longer unusual to find large urban school districts in cities that serve as ports of entry for new immigrants where the number of languages spoken in the homes of the students exceeds fifty. In my own city of Los Angeles, these languages include the mostly oral dialects spoken by indigenous people from Central America as well as the more familiar Spanish, Korean, Mandarin, Thai, Filipino, and Armenian. For the children of these newcomer families, the country of origin remains an important influence. They may have family still living in the highlands of Guatemala, a refugee camp in Thailand, or a village in Bosnia. The connections are still vital.

It is easy to see that the children whose families maintain their international connections are living in a global village. I suggest that other children, like my grandchildren who are now fourth-generation Americans, are also residents in one global village. The ecological and economic and geopolitical realities of the twenty-first century place them there. The library can help prepare them to be more competent and compassionate global citizens.

Our materials collections serve us well as a resource in this endeavor. I still have the copy of Paul Hazard's *Books, Children, and Men* that I bought when I was in library school. I was taken with his notion of the world republic of childhood. This French scholar wrote eloquently about the capacity of books to connect children to one another across national borders.

> Yes, children's books keep alive a sense of nationality; but they also keep alive a sense of humanity. They describe their native land lovingly, but they also describe faraway lands where unknown brothers live. They understand the essential quality of their own race; but each of them is a messenger that goes beyond mountains and rivers, beyond the seas, to the very ends of the world in search of new friendships. Every country gives and every country receives—innumerable are the exchanges— and so it comes about that in the first impressionable years the universal republic of childhood is born. (Hazard 1944, 146)

American cultural hegemony is so strong that it is much more likely that a child living in France, Korea, or Kenya will read a book about the United States than that an American child will read a book that originated in one of those countries. In Croatia, I found "American corners" in many public libraries. Books selected by the U.S. State Department about life in America for children, teens, and adults were donated to some of the larger public libraries there. I had feared that I would see obvious propaganda, but the children's books were well chosen, representing fine writing and illustration as well as the diversity of our population. Children in Croatia start learning English in the early primary grades, so the books are read.

Books in languages other than English are most likely to be found in children's collections serving large immigrant populations. They are well used by children who haven't learned English yet and by families who hope to keep the mother tongue alive even as the children become fluent in English. I have found, however, that even monolingual American children are intrigued with books in other languages. They are especially fascinated by different alphabets. I'm not sure what an American child learns about Japan when she leafs through a Japanese picture book, but it can't hurt to be exposed to the notion that not everybody reads from left to right in the roman alphabet.

Realistically, children are more likely to be exposed to the world republic of childhood through books translated from other languages or books about other countries and cultures that are written in English. There are some useful resources for librarians wishing to augment their collections. The United States Board on Books for Young People (USBBY), for example, compiles an annual list of recommended books from and about other countries. In the introduction to this year's list, Carolyn Angus says the intent is to introduce children to "outstanding authors and illustrators from other countries, help them see the world from other points of view, and provide another perspective or address a topic that may be missing from children's books in the United States" (2009, 36). USBBY has also published three extensive bibliographies that are organized by country so it is possible to identify children's books about specific countries. The most recent volume, *Crossing Boundaries with Children's Books*, edited by Doris Gebel (2006) is not limited to translated books. It also includes books written in the United States but set in another country.

Of course, books are not the only means of connecting children to their brothers and sisters around the world. Electronic resources such as Google Earth are fascinating to many children. Some of the best informational websites offer reliable information on world cultures and religions as well as country data, although children are unlikely to access these sites unless motivated by a homework assignment.

There are many ways that libraries can incorporate international themes and resources into their programming. We already do this with storytelling. Many libraries celebrate holidays such as Cinco de Mayo and the Chinese New Year with cultural programs, often involving traditional food, music, or dance. Certainly holidays are obvious hooks for fostering international awareness, but there are other things we can do as well. We can invite the AFS exchange students attending the local high school to tell about experiences in their home countries. Ask immigrant parents to share nursery rhymes and fingerplays at family storytime. See if you can establish an electronic pen pal relationship between the children at your library and children at a library overseas.

If we begin to think of the American children we serve as citizens in the world republic of childhood who will grow up to be decision makers in an increasingly interconnected global village, we also add another critical dimension to our understanding of contemporary childhood. We will turn next to the notion of the empowered child.

The Empowered Child

Children have little legal power. They are legally in the custody of their parents until the age of 18. Their parents may legally determine where their children live, what they eat, how they will dress, and even what they may read. They are also legally responsible for the consequences of their children's behavior—from replacing a neighbor's window shattered by a baseball to paying the fines on overdue library books. Children are dependent on their parents by law and in practice. They may depend on their parents to sign them up for soccer or to take them to the library. Even the American Library Association, whose Library Bill of Rights asserts that "a person's right to use a library should not be denied or abridged because of origin, age, background, or views," affirms the right and responsibility of parents to guide their own children's use of the library and its resources and services (ALA 2008).

Given this legal and social reality, what is the justification for empowering children? Why should librarians be advocates for children's rights? Barbara Woodhouse (2004) proposes that we recognize two categories of rights especially for children—needs-based rights and dignity-based rights. Needs-based rights would include positive rights to nurturance, education, medical care, and other goods and services that children need to develop into productive adults. Dignity-based rights, on the other hand, recognize that children are fully human from the time of their birth. Dignity-based rights reflect both the inherent dependence and fragility of children and their developing capacity for participation in decisions that affect their lives. Woodhouse (2004, 235–39) identifies five principles of human rights that could and should be applied to children:

- The equality principle: the right to equal opportunity
- The individualism principle: the right to be treated as a person, not an object
- The empowerment principle: the right to a voice and, sometimes, a choice
- The protection principle: the right of the weak to be protected from the strong

- The privacy principle: the right to protection of intimate relationships

This framework resolves much of the tension that has plagued the issue of children's rights. It acknowledges the child's right to protection as well as the child's right to autonomy. Librarians can contribute to this framework a principled defense of children's right to information and the active dissemination of the information that children need in order to exercise their other rights.

What do we mean by rights? Rosalind Ekman Ladd (1996) is a philosopher who defines rights as justified claims: "Whereas a privilege is something that may be offered or taken away, a right must ordinarily be fulfilled unless the individual whose right it is chooses to waive it" (3). An interesting question for those who advocate empowering children to exercise their rights is whether children are developmentally and cognitively able to do so. Two psychologists (Schmidt and Reppucci 2002) point to several studies of children's capacity to understand their legal rights. These studies build on a model much like Lawrence Kohlberg's model of moral development, documenting a shift from a preconventional law-obeying approach to a conventional law-and-order maintaining worldview to a postconventional law-making orientation. The research suggests that children make the shift from preconventional to conventional thinking about legal matters in adolescence and most do not go beyond that level as adults.

If that research is correct, it may be counterproductive to engage preteen children in the consideration of their legal rights. However, there is some evidence to suggest that children can profitably engage in high-level conversations about their rights when presented as philosophical questions. Gareth Mathews is a philosopher who has written extensively about teaching and talking with children about abstract issues of a philosophical nature. He claims that even very young children can "do" philosophy and that respecting them as thinkers brings at least three rewards. First, it may encourage them to develop lifelong habits of reflection. Second, it may give the adults with whom they share their thoughts a fresh perspective on the world. Finally, having a genuine conversation with a child about ideas that both understand to be perplexing—such as the best way to resolve conflicting claims—can enhance intergenerational relationships (Mathews 2004).

Mathews and a number of other scholars are loosely associated in a multidisciplinary area sometimes called "childhood studies." These scholars are encouraging us to reconsider some of our fundamental assumptions of childhood. They point out that many of our ideas about childhood are based on the Aristotelian notion of the child as a proto-adult, as an unformed organism who has yet to fulfill his destiny, or on Rousseau's notion of children as "noble savages." A new approach to childhood would neither patronize children nor idealize them. Rather, it would see them fully as human beings capable of making moral choices and decisions about their lives. It would see children as self-determining actors who are capable of making up their own minds and taking action as a function of their own wills if adults allow them to do so.

Many of the new scholars who identify with the child studies area talk about the importance of children's "voice" and "agency." By *voice*, they mean children's ability to articulate their needs and rights. By *agency*, they mean children's ability to act on their own behalf. Children are naturally social beings who give voice to their ideas in order to be heard and move others to action (Pufall and Unsworth 2004).

Recently four of my former students (now practicing children's librarians) and I put together a presentation about a hypothetical children's library bill of rights for the fiftieth anniversary observance of the MLIS program at UCLA. We raised two relevant questions:

- How can librarians be advocates for children and their rights?
- How can librarians create a culture of respect for children in the library and the community?

We then proposed two answers or solutions to these questions: the establishment of children's advisory boards and the creation of a children's library bill of rights for particular communities. We believe that these two programmatic initiatives would go far to empower children and, in the words of Pufall and Unsworth, provide an opportunity for their exercise of both voice and agency.

Teen advisory boards are now conventional examples of good practice for young adult library services. Why not extend to younger children this opportunity to participate in discussions about the library services that affect them? I frequently conduct focus groups with children as part of my research. I recently asked groups of nine- and ten-year-olds in Phoenix and Chicago what they liked about their library and what they would like to see changed or added. They liked their librarians, and they liked the books. They liked seeing their friends there. They worried about library fines. They thought it was acceptable that their parents and library policies kept them away from MySpace and Facebook, but they looked forward to exploring those sites when they were older. When they talked about changes they would like to see, they began with very conservative, small things such as more copies of popular books and reduced fines for overdues. Both groups of children then warmed up and went spinning off into what might have appeared as fantastic flights of fancy: a swimming pool, snacks, visits by movie stars. While I listened without offering any judgment or commentary, they voluntarily rejected the swimming pool and the movie star visits as being unrealistic. They wanted to keep the snacks, though.

Those conversations with children are instructive, I think. They demonstrate that children are able to articulate wants and needs in a group setting. They are capable of self-monitoring and judging the practicality of those wants and needs. I would submit that listening carefully to their more fanciful ideas also gives an adult some insight into children's hopes and dreams, whether or not they fit neatly into public library mission statements. Incidentally, when teenagers in Philadelphia were given an opportunity to design the ideal library for their neighborhoods, they also inevitably included a swimming pool and a snack bar. Do all young people have unfulfilled desires to swim and to eat?

It would be a relatively easy matter to start a children's advisory group in any library. Such a group might be sponsored by the adult advisory board or by a Friends group. Initial members could be library "regulars" or representatives chosen by local schools. The librarian could convene the group on a regular basis or just when she needed some expert advice: should the library start a book discussion group for kids? What kinds of prizes should we offer during the summer reading program? What would happen if we did away with time limits on computer use?

The Library Bill of Rights activity is a little more complicated. We suggested a process by which a library could involve groups of children — and others such as teens, adults, and Spanish-speaking patrons — in the development of library bills of rights. One process could begin with an interested group of children coming together and rewriting the Library Bill of Rights in plain language that they all understand. They can then talk about changes or additions they would like to make. When they have produced a document whose language and content they feel good about, the children can organize in teams to present it to other groups of children in their community. After the draft Library Bill of Rights has been discussed in three or four other settings, the original working group meets again to finalize their document based on the feedback they have received.

In the meantime, the other working groups have been going through the same process. When all groups have completed their work, the library holds a community forum. Each working group presents its Library Bill of Rights, all of which are then compiled into a Library Bill of Rights specific to that community and that library.

An alternative process for creating the first draft document that we especially like would be to use the World Café process. This method was used to create the Library Teen Bill of Rights presented in *Teens and Libraries: Getting It Right* (Walter and Meyers 2003, 131 ff). The World Café is an effective way to help a group come to consensus on a complex topic, and you can learn how to conduct your own on its website (www .theworldcafe.com).

The children's librarians—Katherine Adams, Joanna Fabicon, Shana Johnson, and Roger Kelly—and I thought that a number of positive outcomes could be achieved from involving children and other members of their community in the creation of a library bill of rights. Children would be given the opportunity to exercise their voice. They would receive a practical lesson in civics and civic involvement. They would see themselves as active participants in the business of the library and the life of their community. Other people would also see them in this light and perhaps look at children with new respect for their competence.

In addition to the positive outcomes for children, the library would receive valuable feedback from its community. We see this project as an initiative designed to empower people to think about their library in terms of rights and responsibilities, to stimulate discussion about the library, and to foster democratic skills and values. With budget cuts on the table in most communities, this is a particularly good time to engage our library patrons of all ages in conversations about the future of their library. And this is an activity that could be carried out without any expenditure of funds at all.

Both the children's advisory board and the Library Bill of Rights projects have the potential to empower children. Librarians can do still more as advocates for children's rights. We can work even harder than we do now to ensure that the library operates in the best interest of children. Two psychologists concerned with children's rights put it like this: "Advocacy on behalf of children is more than simply the provision of needed services to children. Advocacy efforts represent an attempt to increase the responsiveness and accountability of all institutions affecting children" (Small and Limber 2002, 51). As noted elsewhere in this book, children's librarians have a long tradition of advocacy; and advocacy, along with public relations and networking, is one of the seven core competencies for children's librarians put forth by ALSC. ALA has many useful tools that librarians can use to help them lobby for their services within their communities. The new website, Add It Up (ALA 2009), is particularly well designed and helpful.

Small and Limber (2002) recommend that child advocates, no matter what their discipline or profession, look at the United Nations Convention on the Rights of the Child (UNICEF 2006) as a framework for guiding their work. This important document, adopted by the United Nations in 1989, has been ratified by every country in the world except Somalia and the United States. (The United States signed the document but never had it ratified by the Senate.) Some experts believe that as legally binding international law, it takes precedence over United States law. At any rate, it is a remarkable international consensus on the civil, political, economic, social, and cultural rights of children. It covers just about every aspect of children's lives, and it emphasizes respect for children's dignity. It manages to avoid focus on either protection or self-determination for children, the usual opposing viewpoints, and instead promotes liberty, privacy, and nurturance.

The child as reader, the child of the information age, the child in the community, the global child, or the empowered child? Which child will we target as we plan and deliver library services in our communities? The next chapter will look at ways that we can use good management practices in our efforts to provide library services that are truly in the best interests of the child.

FIVE

Getting It Right for the Children

WE NEED MORE THAN GOOD INTENTIONS IF WE ARE GOING TO GET it right for children in the library. We also need more than the skills and knowledge we have acquired as professional librarians. Getting it right is about more than collection development and programming. It also involves working with the nuts and bolts of management and leadership. Most children's librarians need to use these tools even if they do not have the formal job title of supervisor or manager or coordinator. If they are responsible for service to children in a library, they are de facto managers and leaders.

In this chapter I will suggest some of the nuts and bolts that a children's librarian should have at hand in her or his management and leadership toolbox. One of management's maxims is Leaders do the right thing, and managers do things right (Bennis and Nanus 1986). At times we will be called upon to play each of those roles.

Let's look first at the technical nuts and bolts needed to "do things right" as effective managers. A classic formulation of the tasks of management comes from the golden age of scientific management, an optimistic time when people—mostly men, by the way—worked to develop principles for management that anyone could learn to follow. You may have read *Cheaper by the Dozen* by Frank Gilbreth (1948) in which parents try to raise their family of twelve children according to principles of time and motion study. Gilbreth was one of those early architects of scientific management. Luther Gulick was another. His contribution was the formulation of the acronym POSDCORB (Gulick and Urwick 1937). When broken down into its seven parts, POSDCORB was a tool for structuring and analyzing management tasks. It is still a useful way to think about the work of management. The acronym reflects seven management tasks:

- Planning
- Organizing
- Staffing
- Directing

- Coordinating
- Budgeting
- Reporting

We will look at each task in turn, focusing on ways that librarians can use these nuts and bolts of management to do things right for children.

Planning

It is appropriate that planning comes first in our list of management tasks because it is planning that moves our efforts from the realm of ad hoc activities and knee-jerk responses to rational, intentional action. Planning in the world of organizations has come to mean the formulating of the work to be done and the methods for doing it in order to accomplish the mission of the enterprise. Increasingly, planning includes systematic evaluation of the organization's activities to determine if objectives are being met. If not, corrections may need to be made. It may even be necessary to shift course to a new direction.

Planning is such an integral part of contemporary administration that managers have many different approaches to choose from. I referred earlier in this book, for example, to the planning processes that the Public Library Association has developed to assist library directors in their efforts. The PLA manuals are practical guides. Recently, however, I have been pointing youth services librarians to the outcome-based planning and evaluation (OBPE) model developed by Eliza Dresang, Melissa Gross, and Leslie Edmonds Holt (2006).

I like OBPE because it links planning and evaluation into one integrated process. Its use of outcome-based evaluation makes it a useful guide for librarians who must comply with mandates from funding agencies for this kind of approach. OBPE is similar to the logic model that the Institute of Museum and Library Services recommends its grantees use. Dresang, Gross, and Holt have formulated an approach to planning and evaluation that is rational, systematic, and relatively easy to implement.

The OBPE model has four phases:

1. Gathering information
2. Determining outcomes
3. Developing programs and services
4. Conducting evaluations

Any good planning process starts with an information-gathering phase. Strategic planners sometimes talk about this as the "environmental scan."

Requests for proposals for grants from funding agencies sometimes ask for a community needs assessment. Some business sectors think of this as a marketing study. The intent is the same in all these cases. You need to gather data about and from your community of users that will help you determine what desirable outcomes the library should plan to achieve with its services.

I have consulted with many libraries as they have embarked on planning processes. I have found that effort put into the information-gathering phase pays off in the later stages. There are shortcuts that people can take, of course: quick peeks at census data and test scores from local schools, identification of the schools and other agencies serving children in the community, review of library statistics such as circulation and program attendance. A more thorough approach involves gathering data directly from your library users and nonusers. Conduct a user satisfaction study. Interview some key informants—those people in your community who serve as gatekeepers to significant institutions and groups or who hold key positions as PTA presidents, youth ministers, athletic coaches, or day-care providers. Conduct focus groups with children, parents, and other stakeholders in the lives of young people. Get your children's advisory board involved. Maybe this would be a good time to launch the Library Bill of Rights initiative discussed in chapter 4.

Consider convening a planning work group (PWG) composed of key library staff and community people, including children. When you have completed your information-gathering activities, call your PWG together. Share what you have learned. My experience is that some patterns will leap into the foreground as you analyze your data. There will be some key findings that will inform the next planning phase. You may have learned that there are significant demographic shifts taking place in the community. You may have noticed more Spanish-language signs going up in the local stores; now you learn that the number of Limited English Proficiency students in the schools has increased dramatically. Or perhaps the older adults who were such faithful library users are selling their homes in order to move into senior citizen living arrangements. Young families are replacing them and putting a big strain on the local schools. Perhaps parents are concerned about crime or about dangerous traffic on the streets near the library. Maybe the lack of public transportation makes it difficult for children to come to the library on their own. Do families have access to computers with fast broadband connections, or have people fallen on the other side of the digital divide?

As you talk with people in your community, try to find out what they really want from the library. Librarians from Santa Monica who engaged in a planning process several years ago were surprised to learn that older children and younger teens in what they had always considered a relatively crime-free community looked to the library as a safe place. This surprising insight led to a new way of thinking about what kind of environment the library needed to provide.

The information-gathering phase should lead directly to phase 2, determining outcomes. Are there desirable outcomes that would address issues raised in phase 1 that the library could reasonably try to achieve? Dresang, Gross, and Holt define an outcome as "the change in attitude, behavior, skill, knowledge, or status that occurs for users after a purposeful action on the part of the library and library staff" (2006, 3).

This might be a good point in the planning process to map those five models of the child (reader, information-seeker, community member, global citizen, or empowered active agent) against the data you have collected in phase 1. Do the data point you toward one or more of those models? If so, does this suggest some logical outcomes the library might want to pursue? Low reading scores obviously lead to thinking about the child as reader. An influx of new immigrants might suggest a focus on the global child. The children's own enthusiasm for the planning process might indicate interest in encouraging the empowered child. A technologically sophisticated—or deprived—clientele might lead you to rethink your commitment to the child of the information age.

In any case, good outcomes should be derived from the information you gathered in phase 1. In addition to data about and from your community, you will have considered the library's mission, its policies and past practices, and its resources, both current and potential. You may be engaged in a holistic planning process for your entire children's department or you may be looking at just one segment of your services, such as summer reading or preschool initiatives or after-school homework help. It may be easiest to start with one of the more limited activities if this is your first launch into OBPE.

Dresang, Gross, and Holt provide examples and a case study of the application of OBPE to a technology-based program for school-age children in the St. Louis Public Library. They suggest that you start by identifying the kind of outcome you are thinking about: is it a change in skills, knowledge, behavior, attitude, or status? For the St. Louis technology program, they suggested that a typical behavior outcome description might be "increased independent use of digital resources" while a typical skill outcome might be "ability to use the library catalog" (2006, 100).

The next step is to be a little more specific about what that outcome would look like if it were operationalized. How will you know success? How would you know that a child had demonstrated increased independent use of digital resources or the ability to use the library catalog? For the library catalog outcome, Dresang and her colleagues identified three levels of achievement—basic, intermediate, and advanced—and listed the skills that a child would be able to use at each level. This makes it possible to know when an outcome has been achieved.

Phase 3 is the practical part of the process, the time in which the librarian actually develops and implements programs and services intended to achieve the outcomes that were identified in phase 2. We all know how to produce library programs; the difference here is that we are producing library programs designed to generate particular outcomes in the children or adults who participate in them.

Phase 4 will tell us whether those outcomes have been achieved. The evaluation strategy needs to be developed earlier in the process, simultaneously with the program development in phase 3, because it might involve doing some pre- and post-testing of the participants. For example, if the designated outcome was the ability to use the library catalog, we would want to know what level of ability children had *before* they embarked on the program intended to help them gain this skill. Then we would measure their ability *after* they had participated in the after-school computer club or library workshop in which those skills were taught and practiced.

The OBPE process is not completed until results of the evaluation are analyzed and used to determine the effectiveness of the program. The end of phase 4 should lead right back to phase 1 as you consider whether the environmental conditions that led you to decide that this was a desired outcome still exist or whether you need to continue to provide the intervention. If the need still exists but your program did not achieve its desired outcomes, perhaps you need to rethink the program.

It can all sound a little daunting until you have actually worked your way through it, step by step. My students who have learned the process in class tell me that they apply it in many different contexts in the real world, including personal life decisions. After a while it becomes second nature to remember to start with outcomes and work back to programs and services and to build evaluation into the program.

Organizing

Organizing means getting the work done efficiently and effectively. Most librarians are good at efficiency. Our professional education, with its emphasis on organizing information, hones our natural inclinations to orderliness. Effectiveness comes a little harder to all of us. It requires constant monitoring to be sure that all of our orderly actions aimed at accomplishing set routines are actually producing desired results. Fortunately, more attention to planning and evaluating can help us prioritize and focus our work for greater effectiveness.

Given the complexity of most library operations, many children's librarians find that time management is the most important skill they need to acquire. Some people multitask comfortably; others need to focus on one thing at a time. Knowing which approach works for you will help you organize your work.

Staffing

Staffing involves having the right people on hand to do the work and ensuring that they have the resources they need to do their jobs. If you are in a management position, you may be responsible for many people in many job classifications and organizational levels, and staffing—or personnel-related work—may be the major part of your responsibilities. Even beginning children's librarians, however, often find themselves supervising pages or volunteers who work in the children's department.

Training may be the most important resource supervisors can supply. Many library systems offer excellent training opportunities for their members, but you can also do a good job in-house. One of the most effective training programs I have come across is Everybody Serves Youth, developed originally at Multnomah County (Oregon) Library and then carried to Brooklyn Public Library by Ginnie Cooper when she became director there. This workshop curriculum applies basic youth development principles to library services. It is intended for *all* staff, from custodians and security guards to top administrators. Based on evaluations we conducted for the Wallace-funded "Learning in Libraries" project in the three New York library systems in 2006, it works. Staff respond with a renewed appreciation for young people and what the library can do to help them.

Some soft skills can facilitate personnel work: people skills and creativity. A strong stomach and thick skin help when you must handle disciplinary issues. It is also essential to know the ground rules: what civil service rules and personnel policies apply?

I found that nurturing the people who worked for me always paid off. I was lucky in being able to hire people who balanced my limited skills with ample skills of their own. Remember, good employees make you look good as well.

Directing

All public libraries are bureaucracies, a form of organization that has emerged to enable developed societies like ours to get complex tasks done. It is intended to foster efficiency, all jokes about "red tape" to the contrary. One of its ubiquitous characteristics is the hierarchical chain of command. All of us who work in bureaucracies occupy a place in that chain of command with one or more bosses above us in the chain. They are responsible for our work, so they "tell us what to do." We may have one or more people below us in the chain of command. We are responsible for their work, so we "tell them what to do." This interlocking chain of authority and responsibility ensures that the designated work of the organization gets done.

Of course, we can all think of examples where the chain breaks down. We have all had at least one boss from hell. Learn from that bad example and vow to do better yourself. Directing well means delegating work with clarity and fairness. It requires good communication skills and the ability to follow up.

Coordinating

Coordinating is a close cousin to organizing but with the emphasis on getting people to work together on a common task or goal. These might be coworkers or partners from outside the library. Here the key skills seem to be the ability to negotiate and comfort with ambiguity and uncertainty. My favorite organizational theorist, Karl Weick (1995), reminds us that the world is increasingly unknowable. In this environment, it is often a mistake to get too hung up on final decision making. Instead, cultivate what he calls the art of sensemaking. Look for mutual frames of reference on which to build common actions. Navigate by means of a compass instead of a map. Know where you want to go but be flexible about how you get there. It should be obvious once again that planning can help with this task.

Reporting

Usually reporting means checking in with your boss to let him or her know what you're doing. Often it means writing a formal report of your activities for a funding agency. We would do well, however, to remember to report to our broader constituencies: to our staff, to our patrons, to the stakeholders in our communities. We do good work; let's tell everybody about it! Doing this task well requires communication skills, of course, as well as time and knowledge of your own organizational culture and what messages will play well. It might also be a good idea to remember what Malcolm Gladwell said about stickiness: "For an idea or a service or a product to catch on, it needs to be so memorable that it sticks in the mind and so irresistible that it stirs people to action. There is a simple way to package information that, under the right circumstances, can make it irresistible. All you have to do is find it" (2000, 132).

All that may be required of you is that you keep your boss informed or that you file a set of required statistics on time. You can leverage those reporting activities by adding the memorable stories or messages that will make them stick.

Budgeting

Budgeting is really just making sure that you have the resources you need to do your job. We are accustomed to thinking of this in terms of dollars and cents, funds that are funneled into materials or personnel or operating budgets. Large library systems have accounting and business offices that are charged with managing those funds after administrative teams have allocated them. Sometimes it seems that all a children's librarian needs to do is buy a good calculator and keep track of the materials budget.

It doesn't take much reflection to realize that this is too simple a picture. Children's librarians generate resources by applying for grants, raising funds from community sources, and working with volunteers. As we look ahead to a period of almost certain resource scarcity, children's librarians will also need to think about doing more with less and being creative with the resources they do have.

POSDCORB has helped us organize the management tools that enable us to do things right. They are the technical skills that keep bureaucracies running and that bureaucracies tend to reward. The leadership skills that guide us to do the right things are a little different. Good leaders can compensate for the impersonal culture of a bureaucracy. The tools for leadership are less concrete than the nuts and bolts of management: things like vision, ethics, values, passion, and commitment. At least one recent book, *Leadership Can Be Taught* (Parks 2005), refutes the notion that leaders are born, not made, and suggests ways that anyone can become a leader with the capacity to foster collective action. Of course, literally hundreds of books are available that claim to be able to turn you into a leader, books with titles like *Resonant Leadership* (Boyatzis and McKee 2005), *Leading Minds* (Gardner 1995), or even *The Leadership Secrets of Attila the Hun* (Roberts 1990).

I do believe that dipping into business literature can stimulate new ways of thinking about how we can be leaders, whether we hold official positions of power or not. Sample the *Harvard Business Review* and the *Wall Street Journal*. Find out what books have influenced your boss, your mentor, your city manager, or someone you admire. Consider taking a management class or even getting a master's degree in management or public administration.

The book that I go back to over and over again when I need to remind myself that authentic leadership is an attainable goal is *Leaders: Strategies for Taking Charge* (Bennis and Nanus 1986). This influential book still resonates for me more than twenty years after I first read it. Here are some of the key messages from that book that have informed my own approach to leading people in a variety of settings, from the Los Angeles Public Library to the Association for Library Service to Children to the Information Studies Department at UCLA.

Bennis and Nanus postulate four strategies for being an effective leader:

- Attention through vision: The authors are talking here about creating a focus for your work, about being results-oriented or, as I like to think currently, outcomes-oriented.

- Meaning through communication: The authors advocate telling stories about your organization, the people who work there, and the work you do. We children's librarians know how to do this!

- Trust through positioning: We can achieve credibility and accountability by making our position clear and staying the course.

- The deployment of self through positive self-regard: This is not egomaniacal self-importance or self-centeredness. Instead it is knowing yourself well enough that you can recognize your strengths and compensate for your weaknesses.

Bennis and Nanus also identify five key skills for any leader:

- Accept people as they are, not as you would like them to be.
- Approach relationships and problems in terms of the present rather than the past.
- Treat those who are close to you with the same courteous attention that you extend to strangers and casual acquaintances.
- Trust others, even if the risk is great.
- Do without constant approval and recognition from others.

Don't you wish that your boss had read the book, followed the four strategies, and practiced the five skills?

Getting it right for children in the library takes all the management skills and leadership capacity and political savvy that we can muster. The good news is that we are smart, reflective practitioners who are mindful of the consequences of our actions at work. We are accustomed to adapting our practice as circumstances change. When mothers stop bringing children to the morning preschool story hour because they have gone back to work, we invite their nannies to bring the kids or we shift the storytime to an early evening hour. When the local schools go to year-round scheduling, we drop the summer reading program in favor of a year-round reading club. When the after-school crowd threatens to take over every seat in the library, we turn the place into a homework center from three to five o'clock and recruit volunteers to help with schoolwork or read to the younger children.

All we need to do to leverage our natural inclination to get it right is to hone a few of our skills and learn to think like managers through reading or taking classes or just paying attention to the people above us in the chain of command. You can learn from the bad examples as well as the good ones.

Good management and leadership skills will help us get it right for children today. We also have an obligation to lay the groundwork for their future and for the children of tomorrow. In the next chapter, we will think about claiming the future for library services to children.

SIX

Claiming the Future

THE SURRENDER TREE (ENGLE 2008) IS A BOOK OF POEMS THAT TELL the story of Cuba's wars for independence from Spain, fought from 1850 to 1899. It is a much-honored book that received the Pura Belpré Medal for distinguished writing by a Latina author and a Newbery Honor for distinguished writing by an American author. The poems are powerful, and they tell a story that is unfamiliar to many Americans. The dominant voice is that of Rosa, a slave who escaped to the forest and joined the freedom fighters there. She uses her healing skills and knowledge of medicinal plants to ease the pain and suffering of wounded men on both sides of the fighting. A young girl named Silvia escapes from the reconcentration camps established by the Spanish government to control the peasant population of the island. She joins Rosa, who has grown old while the wars rage on endlessly. Rosa teaches Silvia one cure at a time. She introduces her to the *Simple Verses* of José Marti, the poet who first inspired her to hope, and watches as the young woman becomes a healer in her own right. Rosa thinks that she and her husband are like the rock-hard wood of the *guayacan* tree, so heavy that it cannot float, while young people are like the wood of a balsa tree, light and airy.

> Young people drift on airy daydreams.
> Old folks help hold them in place. (113)

It is our responsibility as adults to be the anchors for the next generation's dreams and dreamers, not to hold them back but to lift them up. It is really the children who will claim the future, but we must ensure that they are given the supports and opportunities that will enable them to do so with hope and joy and a sense of their rightful entitlement.

Children's librarians are privileged to be given the opportunity to spend their workdays with young people. We know how funny and poignant, how joyful and despairing, how clever and struggling those young people can be. We take them as they come and value them as they are, not for the adults they will become. They remind us of ourselves when we were young, and at the same time we marvel at the changes in the world they live in. We are privileged to work for a public institution that enjoys the respect and support of its stakeholders, including those young people and the significant adults in their lives: parents, day-care providers, teachers, and so many others who join us in a web of support for children and their families.

This is the last chapter in the book. However, it also represents the beginning of a new conversation about children and libraries. I hope that it raises as many questions as it answers and that it generates countless conversations between concerned adults inside and outside our profession and between caring adults and children. Here are some questions that might start those conversations:

- How do children define community?
- Can the library generate communities of child readers? Communities of child gamers? Intergenerational communities? Global communities? Virtual communities?
- Can the library provide a haven for the solitary child reader as well as the child looking for connections with other like-minded people?
- What do children need to be "good at being kids"? Can the library provide solutions for any of these needs?
- What do children need now that will enable them to move successfully through adolescence and into adulthood? Can the library provide solutions for any of these needs?
- Look again at the five constructs of childhood presented in this book: child as reader, child of the information age, child in the community, global child, and empowered child. Which of these models provides the theoretical or philosophical underpinning for your library's service to children? Why? Would there be any value in shifting the model, or in adding one or more?
- What would be the consequences for the children in your community if the library suddenly went away?
- And, of course, how are the children?

We cannot know the future, but we can be sure that getting there will not be easy. Our libraries face economic pressures unlike any we have seen in recent times. Our children will experience decreased funding in all of the institutions that affect them most—schools, parks and recreation facilities, and, of course, their public libraries. Many will also experience shrinking family budgets. They inherit an unhealthy and rapidly deteriorating ecological environment and a world of people who cannot find a way to live peacefully with their neighbors. We can only hope that we are giving our children the firm foundation that will enable them to solve problems, face challenges, and live in peace and harmony. We must be like Rosa, as rock-hard and firm as the *guayacan* tree.

I ended *Children and Libraries: Getting It Right* (2001) with a paragraph that was intended to remind readers why we do what we do for children. It still rings true for me so I will repeat those words to close this book.

We must keep our eyes on the prize. The goal is good libraries for the children of today and better libraries for the children of tomorrow. We must constantly remember what excellent library services can do for children. We give children hope, dreams, words to think with, inspiration, information, positive role models, cultural validation, self-esteem, personal attention, a listening ear, opportunities to participate in the life of their community, moments of delight, answers to questions, and questions to answer. What other public agency can offer so much?

REFERENCES

Agosto, Denise. 2008. The Lubuto Library Project and the universality of public library services for youth. *Public Libraries* 47 (6): 56–60.

ALA American Library Association. 2008. Free access to libraries for minors: An interpretation of the Library Bill of Rights. Chicago: ALA. www.ala .org/ala/aboutala/offices/oif/statementspols/statementsif/interpretations/ freeaccesslibraries.cfm (accessed February 13, 2009).

———. n.d. The Children's Internet Protection Act (CIPA). Chicago: ALA. www .ala.org/ala/aboutala/offices/wo/woissues/civilliberties/cipaweb/cipa.cfm (accessed July 20, 2009).

ALA American Library Association, Office for Library Advocacy. 2009. Add it up: Libraries make the difference in youth development and education. Chicago: ALA. www.ala.org/ala/issuesadvocacy/advocacy/advocacyuniversity/additup/ index.cfm (accessed February 13, 2009).

ALSC Association for Library Service to Children. 1999. Competencies for Librarians Serving Children in Public Libraries, Revised Edition. Chicago: ALSC. www.ala.org/ala/mgrps/divs/alsc/edcareeers/alsccorecomps/index.cfm (accessed January 12, 2009).

———. n.d.-a. Batchelder Award Winners, 1968–Present. Chicago: ALSC. www .ala.org/ala/mgrps/divs/alsc/awardsgrants/bookmedia/batchelderaward/batch elderpast/index.cfm (accessed January 22, 2009).

———. n.d.-b. Great Technology Programs for Children. Chicago: ALSC. http:// wikis.ala.org/alsc/index.php/Great_Technology_Programs_for_Children (accessed February 7, 2009).

———. n.d.-c. Great Web Sites for Kids. Chicago: ALSC. www.ala.org/greatsites/ (accessed February 7, 2009).

———. n.d.-d. Newbery Medal and Honor Books, 1922–Present. Chicago: ALSC. www.ala.org/ala/mgrps/divs/alsc/awardsgrants/bookmedia/newberymedal/ newberyhonors/newberymedal.cfm (accessed July 20, 2009).

ALSC Association for Library Service to Children and PLA Public Library Association. 2003. Every Child Ready to Read @ your library pilot project

2003 evaluation. Chicago: ALSC and PLA. www.ala.org/ala/mgrps/divs/alsc/ecrr/projecthistory/pilotprojectevaluation/evaluationreport/evalreport.cfm (accessed July 20, 2009).

Anderson, Richard C., E. H. Hiebert, J. A. Scott, and I. A. G. Wilkinson. 1985. *Becoming a nation of readers: The report of the Commission on Reading.* Washington, DC: U.S. Department of Education, National Institute of Education.

Angus, Carolyn. 2009. World class. *School Library Journal* 55 (2): 36–39.

Bader, Barbara. 1997. Only the best: The hits and misses of Anne Carroll Moore. *Horn Book* 73 (5): 520–28.

Batchelder, Mildred L. 1972. Translations of children's books. *Minnesota Libraries* (Autumn): 307–15.

Beck, John C., and Mitchell Wade. 2004. *Got game: How the gamer generation is reshaping business forever.* Boston: Harvard Business School Press.

Bennis, Warren, and Burt Nanus. 1986. *Leaders: Strategies for taking charge.* New York: HarperBusiness.

Benton Foundation. 1996. *Buildings, books, and bytes: Libraries and communities in the digital age.* Washington, DC: Benton Foundation.

Borgman, Christine L., Sandra G. Hirsh, Virginia A. Walter, and A. L. Gallagher. 1995. Children's searching behavior on browsing and keyword online catalogs: The Science Library Catalog. *Journal of the American Society for Information Science* 46 (9): 663–84.

Bostwick, Arthur E. 1913. A volume of children's work in the United States. *ALA Bulletin* 7 (July): 287–91.

Boyatzis, Richard, and Annie McKee. 2005. *Resonant leadership: Renewing yourself and connecting with others through mindfulness, hope, and compassion.* Boston: Harvard Business School Press.

Chelton, Mary K. 1980. Evaluating the impact of federally funded public library youth programs. In *Library programs: Evaluating federally funded public library programs,* ed. Betty Turock, 55–65. Washington, DC: Superintendent of Documents, U.S. Government Printing Office.

Children's Partnership. 2007. Helping our children succeed: What's broadband got to do with it? *Digital Opportunity for Youth Issue Brief,* no. 1. 2nd ed. (March).

Chmielewski, Dawn C. 1999. Public access. *Orange County Register,* July 27, 9.

Connor, Jane Gardner. 1990. *Children's library services handbook.* Phoenix, AZ: Oryx Press.

Copple, Carol, and Sue Bredekamp. 2009. *Developmentally appropriate practice in early childhood programs serving children from birth through age 8.* Washington, DC: National Association for the Education of Young Children.

Cummins, Julie. 1999. More than meets the eye. *School Library Journal* 45 (7): 27–29.

Dresang, Eliza T. 1999. *Radical change: Books for youth in a digital age.* New York: H. W. Wilson.

———. 2005. The information-seeking behavior of youth in the digital environment. *Library Trends* 54 (2): 178–96.

Dresang, Eliza T., Melissa Gross, and Leslie E. Holt. 2006. *Dynamic youth services through outcome-based planning and evaluation.* Chicago: American Library Association.

Druin, Allison. 2005. Introduction. *Library Trends* 54 (2): 173–77.

Eastman, Linda A. 1929. Looking backward and forward. In *Children's library yearbook 1929.* Chicago: American Library Association.

Eddy, Jacalyn. 2006. *Bookwomen: Creating an empire in children's book publishing 1919–1939.* Madison: University of Wisconsin Press.

Engle, Margarita. 2008. *The surrender tree: Poems of Cuba's struggle.* New York: Holt.

Fasick, Adele. 1990. Research and measurement in library services to children. In *Evaluation strategies and techniques for public library children's services: A sourcebook,* ed. Jane Robbins. Madison: University of Wisconsin, School of Library and Information Studies.

Federal Communications Commission. 2008. Children's Internet Protection Act. www.fcc.gov/cgb/consumerfacts/cipa.html (accessed July 18, 2008).

Feinberg, Sandra, Joan F. Kuchner, and Sari Feldman. 1998. *Learning environments for young children: Rethinking library spaces and services.* Chicago: American Library Association.

Fenwick, Sara Innis. 1976. Library service to children and young people. *Library Trends* 25 (1): 329–60.

Fisher, Karen E., Elizabeth Marcoux, Eric Meyers, and Carol F. Landry. 2007. Tweens and everyday life information behavior: Preliminary findings from Seattle. In *Youth information-seeking behavior II,* ed. Mary K. Chelton and Colleen Cool, 1–25. Lanham, MD: Scarecrow Press.

Fletcher, William I. 1876. Public libraries and the young. In *Public libraries in the United States: Their history, condition and management.* Washington, DC: Department of the Interior, Bureau of Education.

Garcia, June, and Sandra Nelson. 2007. *Public library service responses 2007.* Chicago: Public Library Association.

Gardner, Howard E. 1995. *Leading minds: An anatomy of leadership.* New York: Basic Books.

Gebel, Doris, ed. 2006. *Crossing boundaries with children's books.* Lanham, MD: Scarecrow Press.

Gilbreth, Frank. 1948. *Cheaper by the dozen*. New York: Crowell.

Gladwell, Malcolm. 2000. *The tipping point: How little things can make a big difference*. Boston: Little, Brown.

Goldhor, Herbert, ed. 1997. Buildings, books, and bytes: Perspectives on the Benton Foundation Report on Libraries in a Digital Age. *Library Trends* 46 (1): 1–228.

Gross, Melissa. 2006. *Studying children's questions: Imposed and self-generated information seeking at school*. Lanham, MD: Scarecrow Press.

Gulick, Luther, and Lyndall Urwick, eds. 1937. *Papers on the science of administration*. New York: Institute of Public Administration.

Hawes, Joseph M. 1991. *The children's rights movement: A history of advocacy and protection*. Boston: Twayne.

Hazard, Paul. 1944. *Books, children, and men*. Boston: Horn Book.

Hearne, Betsy, and Christine Jenkins. 1999. Sacred texts: What our foremothers left us in the way of psalms, proverbs, precepts, and practices. *Horn Book* 75 (5): 536–58.

Institute of Museum and Library Services. 2008. Grant Search. Washington, DC: IMLS. www.imls.gov/search.asp (accessed July 5, 2008).

International Youth Library. n.d. www.ijb.de/files/english/HMe_1/Page01.htm (accessed February 1, 2009).

Jenkins, Christine A. 1996. Women of ALA youth services and professional jurisdiction: Of nightingales, Newberies, realism, and the right books, 1937–1945. *Library Trends* 44 (4): 813–39.

Johnson, Steven. 2005. *Everything bad is good for you: How today's popular culture is actually making us smarter*. New York: Riverhead Books.

Kanter, Rosabeth Moss. 1994. Collaborative advantage: The art of alliances. *Harvard Business Review* 72 (4): 96–108.

Kenney, Brian. 2009. Happy days. *School Library Journal* 55 (1): 28–31.

Krashen, Stephen D. 2004. *The power of reading: Insights from the research*. 2nd ed. Westport, CT: Libraries Unlimited; Portsmouth, NH: Heinemann.

Kruse, Ginny Moore. 2008. The ALSC Mildred L. Batchelder Award for Translated Children's Books. Chicago: Association for Library Service to Children. www.ala.org/ala/mgrps/divs/alsc/awardsgrants/bookmedia/batchelderaward/batchelderhist/batchelderaward.cfm (accessed January 22, 2009).

Ladd, Rosalind Ekman. 1996. *Children's rights re-visioned: Philosophical readings*. Belmont, CA: Wadsworth.

Large, Andrew, and Jamshid Beheshti. 2005. Interface design, web portals, and children. *Library Trends* 54 (2): 318–42.

Leigh, Robert D. 1950. *The public library in the United States*. New York: Columbia University Press.

Lepman, Jella. 1969. *A bridge of children's books*. Leicester, UK: Brockhampton Press.

Lepore, Jill. 2008. The lion and the mouse. *The New Yorker*, July 21. www.new yorker.com/reporting/2008/07/21/080721fa_fact_lepore (accessed January 4, 2008).

Levitt, Steven D., and Stephen J. Dubner. 2005. *Freakonomics: A rogue economist explores the hidden side of everything*. Rev. and exp. ed. New York: Morrow.

Literary reading in dramatic decline, according to National Endowment for the Arts survey. 2004. Washington, DC: National Endowment for the Arts. www.nea.gov/news/news04/ReadingAtRisk.html (accessed February 2, 2009).

Lu, Ya-Ling. 2008. Coping assistance vs. readers' advisory: Are they the same animal? *Children and Libraries* 6 (11): 15–22.

Lundin, Anne. 1996. The pedagogical context of women in children's services and literature scholarship. *Library Trends* 44 (4): 840–50.

———. 1998. Anne Carroll Moore (1871–1961): I have spun out a long thread. In *Reclaiming the American library past: Writing the women in*, ed. Suzanne Hildenbrand. Norwood, NJ: Ablex.

Maack, Mary Niles. 1993. L'Heure Joyeuse, the first children's library in France: Its contribution to a new paradigm for public libraries. *Library Quarterly* 63 (3): 257–81.

Marcus, Leonard S. 2008. *Minders of make-believe: Idealists, entrepreneurs, and the shaping of American children's literature*. Boston: Houghton Mifflin.

Mathews, Gareth. 2004. Children as philosophers. In *Rethinking childhood*, ed. Peter B. Pufall and Richard P. Unsworth, 38–53. New Brunswick, NJ: Rutgers University Press.

McClure, Charles R., et al. 1987. *Planning and role setting for public libraries*. Chicago: American Library Association.

McElderry, Margaret K. 1997. Remarkable women: Anne Carroll Moore and company. In *School Library Journal's best: A reader for children's, young adult, and school librarians*, ed. Lillian N. Gerhardt. New York: Neal-Schuman.

Mediavilla, Cindy. 2001. *Creating the full-service homework center in your library*. Chicago: American Library Association.

Melcher, Frederic G. 1929. Thirty years of children's books. In *Children's library yearbook 1929*. Chicago: American Library Association.

Miller, Laura. 2008. *The magician's book: A skeptic's adventures in Narnia*. New York: Little, Brown.

Molz, Redmond Kathleen, and Phyllis Dain. 1999. *Civic space/cyberspace: The American public library in the information age*. Cambridge, MA: MIT Press.

Mondowney, JoAnn G. 1997. Licensed to learn: Drivers' training for the Internet. *School Library Journal* 42 (1): 32–34.

Moore, Anne Carroll. 1929. Modern tendencies in books for children. In *Children's library yearbook 1929*. Chicago: American Library Association.

———. 1969. *My roads to childhood: Views and reviews of children's books*. Boston: Horn Book.

More American adults read literature according to new NEA study. 2009. Washington, DC: National Endowment for the Arts. www.nea.gov/news/news09/ReadingonRise.html (accessed February 2, 2009).

Olcott, Frances Jenkins. 1905. Rational library work with children and the preparation for it. In *Proceedings of the American Library Association Conference*, 71–75. Chicago: American Library Association.

Osborne, David, and Ted Gaebler. 1992. *Reinventing government: How the entrepreneurial spirit is transforming the public sector*. Reading, MA: Addison-Wesley.

Papert, Seymour. 1993. *The children's machine: Rethinking school in the age of the computer*. New York: Basic Books.

Parks, Sharon Daloz. 2005. *Leadership can be taught: A bold approach for a complex world*. Boston: Harvard Business School Press.

Pellowski, Anne. 1990. *The world of storytelling*. Exp. and rev. ed. New York: H. W. Wilson.

PLA Public Library Association. 1997. Public Library Data Service Statistical Report 1997. Chicago: PLA.

Power, Effie L. 1929. Organization and equipment of a children's room. In *Children's library yearbook 1929*. Chicago: American Library Association.

Pufall, Peter B., and Richard P. Unsworth. 2004. The imperative and the process for rethinking childhood. In *Rethinking childhood*, ed. Peter B. Pufall and Richard P. Unsworth, 1–21. New Brunswick, NJ: Rutgers University Press.

Riechel, Rosemarie. 1991. *Reference services for children and young adults*. Hamden, CT: Library Professional Publications.

Roberts, Wess. 1990. *The leadership secrets of Attila the Hun*. New York: Warner Books.

Rollock, Barbara T. 1988. *Public library services for children*. Hamden, CT: Library Professional Publications.

Sayers, Frances Clarke. 1965. Lose not the nightingale. In *Summoned by books: Essays and speeches by Frances Clarke Sayers*, comp. Marjeanne Jensen Blinn, 52–67. New York: Viking.

———. 1972. *Anne Carroll Moore*. New York: Atheneum.

Schmidt, Melinda G., and N. Dickon Reppucci. 2002. Children's rights and capacities. In *Children, social science, and the law*, ed. Bette L. Bottoms, Margaret Bull Kovera, and Bradley D. McAuliff, 76–105. New York: Cambridge University Press.

Schwartz, Lynne Sharon. 1997. *Ruined by reading*. Boston: Beacon Press.

Shenton, Andrew. 2007. Causes of information failure: Some insights from an English research project. In *Youth information-seeking behavior II: Context, theories, models, and issues*, ed. Mary K. Chelton and Colleen Cool, 313–64. Lanham, MD: Scarecrow Press.

Silvey, Anita. 2008. Has the Newbery lost its way? *School Library Journal*, October 1. www.schoollibraryjournal.com/article/CA6601546.html (accessed August 5, 2009).

Small, Mark A., and Susan P. Limber. 2002. Advocacy for children's rights. In *Children, social science, and the law*, ed. Bette L. Bottoms, Margaret Bull Kovera, and Bradley D. McAuliff, 51–75. New York: Cambridge University Press.

Staerkel, Kathleen, Mary Fellows, and Sue McCleaf Nespeca. 1995. *Youth services librarians as managers: A how-to guide from budgeting to personnel*. Chicago: American Library Association/Association of Library Service to Children.

Sullivan, Michael. 2005. *Fundamentals of children's services*. Chicago: American Library Association.

Thomas, Fannette H. 1990. Early appearances of children's reading rooms in public libraries. *Journal of Youth Services* 4:81–85.

UNICEF. 2006. Convention on the Rights of the Child: Protecting and Realizing Children's Rights. www.unicef.org/crc/index_protecting.html (accessed January 28, 2009).

Upon the objects to be attained by the establishment of a public library: Report of the trustees of the Public Library of the City of Boston. 1852. Boston: Trustees of the Public Library of the City of Boston.

Van House, Nancy, et al. 1987. *Output measures for public libraries: A manual of standardized procedures*. 2nd ed. Chicago: American Library Association.

Van Slyck, Abigail A. 1995. *Free to all: Carnegie libraries and American culture 1890–1920*. Chicago: University of Chicago Press.

Vandergrift, Kay. 1996. Female advocacy and harmonious voices: A history of public library services and publishing for children in the United States. *Library Trends* 44 (4): 683–718.

Walter, Virginia A. 1992. *Output measures for public library service to children: A manual of standardized procedures*. Chicago: American Library Association.

———. 1994. The information needs of children. *Advances in Librarianship* 40:111–29.

———. 1995. *Output measures and more: Planning and evaluating public library services for young adults*. Chicago: American Library Association.

———. 1997. Becoming digital: Policy implications for library youth services. *Library Trends* 45 (4): 585–601.

———. 2001. *Children and libraries: Getting it right*. Chicago: American Library Association.

———. 2008. Information literacy: A new role for public libraries? In *Proven strategies for building a successful information literacy program*, ed. Sue Curzon and Lynn Lampert, 297–307. New York: Neal-Schuman.

Walter, Virginia A., and Christine Borgman. 1991. The Science Library Catalog: A prototype information retrieval system for children. *Journal of Youth Services in Libraries* 4 (2): 159–66.

Walter, Virginia A., Cindy Mediavilla, Linda Braun, and Elaine Meyers. 2005. *Learning in libraries: White paper on principles and practices for public library services to children and young adults during out-of-school time*. Evanston, IL: Urban Libraries Council.

Walter, Virginia A., and Elaine Meyers. 2003. *Teens and libraries: Getting it right*. Chicago: American Library Association.

Weick, Karl E. 1995. *Sensemaking in organizations*. Thousand Oaks, CA: Sage.

Willett, Holly G. 1995. *Public library youth services: A public policy approach*. Norwood, NJ: Ablex.

Williams, Patrick. 1988. *The American public library and the problem of purpose*. New York: Greenwood.

Wishy, Bernard. 1968. *The child and the republic: The dawn of modern American child nurture*. Philadelphia: University of Pennsylvania Press.

Wolf, Maryanne. 2007. *Proust and the squid: The story and science of the reading brain*. New York: HarperCollins.

Woodhouse, Barbara. 2004. Re-visioning rights for children. In *Rethinking childhood*, ed. Peter B. Pufall and Richard P. Unsworth, 229–43. New Brunswick, NJ: Rutgers University Press.

INDEX

E

early literacy programs
    facilities for, 21
    and library buildings, 33–34
    and parents, 26–27, 31–32, 56, 66
    and story hours, 29
Eastman, Linda A., 8
economic downturn, effect of, 55, 89
ECRR (Every Child Ready to Read @ your
    library), 27, 32, 56
Edwards, Margaret A., 6
effectiveness of organizing, 82
electronic resources, 16–17, 59–64, 70
empowered child, 71–76
empowerment of reading, 55
Enoch Pratt Public Library (Baltimore,
    MD), 61–62
environmental scan in planning process,
    78–79
equal opportunity, right to, 71
evaluation of services
    history, 11–15
    in outcome-based planning and evalua-
      tion, 78, 81
evaluation of websites, instruction in, 62–63
Every Child Ready to Read @ your library
    (ECRR), 27, 32, 56
Everybody Serves Youth training program, 82
experience, expansion of, 55

F

Family Place Libraries, 21, 34
federal aid to libraries, effect of, 10
feminism in children's librarianship, 6
filtering of Internet, 17–18, 37
Fletcher, William I., 1–2, 21
focus for work, creation of, 85
focus groups, 73–74, 79
foreign language materials, 69–70
founding mothers
    promotion of reading by, 28
    values of, 22–23
"Four Respects," 5, 35
frames of reference, shared, 55
French libraries, 51
friendly attitude toward children, 7
funding and partnerships, 47
fund-raising, 84

G

Gail Borden Public Library (Elgin, IL), 63
game playing, 59–60

Geisel Medal, 25
German libraries, 51
Gilbreth, Frank, 77
global child, 67–71
global perspective, need for, 23, 49–53
global warming, 68
Google, 61
grants, 84
groups of children, interaction with, 31
Gulick, Luther, 77

H

Hall, G. Stanley, 2
Hazard, Paul, 6, 69
health care and computer access, 60
Hennepin County (MN) Library, 63
Hewins, Caroline, 5
homework centers
    development of, 33
    guidance on use of digital resources, 18,
      43–44
    and latchkey children, 31

I

IBBY (International Board on Books for
    Young People), 51
IFLA (International Federation of Library
    Associations and Institutions), 52–53
imagination in children's reading, 24
ImaginOn (Public Library of Charlotte and
    Mecklenburg County, NC), 20
IMLS (Institute of Museum and Library
    Services), 10–11, 45
immigrants in community, 68–69
imposed queries, 31, 40–41
individual child as primary user of
    children's library service
    as core value, 22, 30–32
    readers' advisory for, 30
    and right to be treated as a person, 71,
      86
    as solitary reader, 88
    uniqueness of children, 7
information gathering in planning process,
    78–79
information literacy instruction in public
    libraries, 18, 43–44, 62–63
information seeking by children, 40–42
information services
    in addition to pleasure reading, 23
    measures of, 13
    role of, 39–44

Institute of Museum and Library Services
(IMLS), 10–11, 45
intellectual freedom
advocacy for, 37–38
and civic role of libraries, 48
and filtering, 18, 37
International Board on Books for Young
People (IBBY), 51
International Federation of Library Associations and Institutions (IFLA), 52–53
international libraries, 49–53
International Youth Library (Munich,
Germany), 51
Internet
filtering, 17–18
increase in services, 16–17
instruction in evaluation of, 18, 62–63
See also computers

K

keyboarding skills and information seeking,
42

L

Ladd, Rosalind Ekman, 72
latchkey children, 30–31
Leaders: Strategies for Taking Charge (Bennis and Namus), 85
leadership skills, 85
legal rights of children, 72
Lepman, Jella, 51
L'Heure Joyeuse, 51
library as place
design of children's room, 32
as haven for solitary reader, 88
as safe place, 80
See also children's rooms
library as public space and outreach programming, 66
Library Bill of Rights initiatives, 73, 74–75,
79
library buildings, 16, 18–20. *See also* library
as place
library education for children's librarians,
4, 36
library instruction in public libraries, 18,
43–44, 62–63
Library Services and Construction Act
(LSCA), 9
Library Services and Technology Act
(LSTA), 10
library use measures, 12

literary development as goal for library, 5
Los Angeles (CA) Public Library, Venice
branch, 66
LSCA (Library Services and Construction
Act), 9
LSTA (Library Services and Technology
Act), 10
Lubuto Library Project (Zambia), 51–52

M

Mahony, Bertha E., 6
managers, children's librarians as, 15, 77
marketing studies in planning process, 79
Maslow's need hierarchy, 40
materials availability measures, 13
materials collections, 69
materials use measures, 12–13
Mathews, Gareth, 72
measures of outcomes, 81
Melcher, Frederic G., 8
Meyers, Jane Kinney, 51–52
Middle Country (NY) Public Library, 21
middle school children, information literacy
of, 63
models of the child. *See* child, concept of
Monrovia (CA) Public Library, 49
Moore, Anne Carroll
background, 4–6, 51
on children's rooms, 3
influence on profession, 35, 36
influence on publishers, 8–9, 24
multiculturalism in Newbery books, 50
multitasking skills and computer games, 60
Multnomah County (OR) Library, 82
Munson, Amelia H., 6
museums in partnership with libraries,
10–11

N

negotiating skills, 83
networking skills, 37, 76
New York Public Library, 50
Newbery Medal, 22, 25, 50
noble savage, child as, 73
non-English-speaking users
and homework centers, 33
ties to country of origin, 69–70

O

OBPE (outcome-based planning and evaluation), 78–81
Olcott, Frances Jenkins, 3, 64

LaVergne, TN USA
09 June 2010
185571LV00007BA/146/P